Magic Johnson

BASKETBALL LEGEND, ENTREPRENEUR, AND HIV/AIDS ACTIVIST

By Diane Dakers

Crabtree Publishing Company

www.crabtreebooks.com

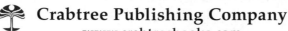

Crabtree Publishing Company
www.crabtreebooks.com

Author: Diane Dakers

Series research and development:
Reagan Miller

Project coordinator: Mark Sachner

Editors: Mark Sachner, Lynn Peppas

Indexer: Gini Holland

Editorial director: Kathy Middleton

Photo research: Mark Sachner and Ruth Owen

Designer: Westgraphix/Tammy West

Proofreader: Wendy Scavuzzo

**Production coordinator and
prepress technician:** Ken Wright

Print coordinator: Kathy Berti

Written and produced by Water Buffalo Books

Publisher's note:
All quotations in this book come from original sources and contain the spelling and grammatical inconsistencies of the original text. Some of the quotations may also contain terms that are no longer in use and may be considered inappropriate or offensive. The use of such terms is for the sake of preserving the historical and literary accuracy of the sources and should not be seen as encouraging or endorsing the use of such terms today.

Photographs and reproductions:
AP Photo: Chris Martinez: p. 81; Al Goldis: p. 94. **Getty Images:** Andrew D. Bernstein: cover (background); Stephen Kim: p. 1; Manny Millan: pp. 8 (bottom), 59; Ronald Martinez: p. 10; Jim Estrin: p. 11; Gary Friedman: pp. 19, 25 (bottom); NBA Photos: pp. 27, 63, 71 (bottom); George Gojkovich: p. 45; Lane Stewart: p. 48; Bettmann: pp. 50 (both), 53 (bottom), 56, 72 (top); Sports Illustrated: pp. 51 (bottom), 77 (bottom); Focus on Sport: p. 65; Bruce Glikas: p. 73; SI Cover: p. 75; John Soohoo: p. 87; Neil Leifer: pp. 88 (bottom), 103; Vince Bucci: p. 90; Jason LaVeris: p. 95; Don Bartletti: p. 99; Victor Decolongon: p. 100 (top). **Library of Congress:** p. 35. **Sara Sachner Elsden:** p. 4. **Public domain:** pp. 7 (bottom), 9 (bottom), 14, 20, 28, 31 (top), 33, 38 (both), 39, 47, 54 (both), 61 (top), 72 (bottom), 82, 100 (bottom), 101. **Shutterstock:** © Joe Seer: p. 8 (top); © Henryk Sadura: p. 17 (bottom); © Dmitriy Bryndin: p. 18 (top); © catwalker: p. 18 (bottom); © xc: pp. 22 (top), 25 (top); © haeton: p. 22 (middle); © Vasilyev Alexandr: p. 22 (bottom); © Ysbrand Cosijn: p. 23 (top); © Jacob Lund: p. 23 (middle); © ssuaphotos: p. 23 (bottom); © EQRoy: p. 42; © Al Sermeno Photography: p. 43; © Andrius Repsys: p. 49; © dean bertoncelj: p. 55; © s_bukley: cover (front) p. 58; © Featureflash Photo Agency: pp. 69 (bottom); 78; © rook76: p. 102. **Superstock:** p. 84; mrk movie / Marka. **Wikipedia/Creative Commons:** © Steve Lipofsky Basketballphoto.com: pp. 5, 17 (top), 41 (top), 51 (top), 53 (top), 61 (bottom), 71 (top), 77 (top), 89, 97; D. Gordon E. Robertson: p. 7 (top); rizha ubal: p. 9 (top); Fred Palumbo/JoeJohnson2: p. 24; Dj1997: p. 31 (bottom); The U.S. Army: p. 34; Infrogmation of New Orleans: p. 41 (left); cbl62: p. 41 (right); Keith Allison: p. 67; Malingering from Los Angeles, CA, USA: p. 69 (top); Howcheng: p. 88 (top).

Library and Archives Canada Cataloguing in Publication

Dakers, Diane, author
   Magic Johnson : basketball legend, entrepreneur, and HIV/AIDS activist / Diane Dakers.
   (Crabtree groundbreaker biographies) Includes index.
Issued in print and electronic formats.
ISBN 978-0-7787-2608-1 (hardback).--ISBN 978-0-7787-2610-4 (paperback).--ISBN 978-1-4271-8102-2 (html)

      1. Johnson, Earvin, 1959- --Juvenile literature. 2. African American basketball players--Biography--Juvenile literature. 3. Basketball players--United States--Biography--Juvenile literature. 4. HIV-positive persons--United States--Biography--Juvenile literature. 5. AIDS activists--United States--Biography--Juvenile literature. I. Title. II. Series: Crabtree groundbreaker biographies

GV884.J63D35 2016   j796.323092   C2016-904174-3
                                                C2016-904175-1

Library of Congress Cataloging-in-Publication Data

Names: Dakers, Diane, author.
Title: Magic Johnson : basketball legend, entrepreneur, and HIV/AIDS activist / Diane Dakers.
Description: New York : Crabtree Publishing, [2016] | Series: Crabtree Groundbreaker Biographies | Includes index.
Identifiers: LCCN 2016031767 (print) | LCCN 2016032351 (ebook) (print) | LCCN 2016032352 (ebook) | ISBN 9780778726081 (Reinforced library binding: alk. paper) | ISBN 9780778726104 (Paperback : alk. paper) | ISBN 9781427181022 (Electronic HTML)
Subjects: LCSH: Johnson, Earvin, 1959---Juvenile literature. | Basketball players--United States--Biography--Juvenile literature. | African American basketball players--Biography--Juvenile literature. | Businessmen--United States--Biography--Juvenile literature. | African American businesspeople--Biography--Juvenile literature.
Classification: LCC GV884.J63 D35 2016 (print) | LCC GV884.J63 (ebook) | DDC 796.323092 [B] --dc23
LC record available at https://lccn.loc.gov/2016031767

Crabtree Publishing Company
www.crabtreebooks.com   1-800-387-7650

Printed in Canada/082016/TL20160715

Published in Canada
Crabtree Publishing
616 Welland Ave.
St. Catharines, Ontario
L2M 5V6

Published in the United States
Crabtree Publishing
PMB16A
350 Fifth Ave., Suite 3308
New York, NY 10118

Published in the United Kingdom
Crabtree Publishing
Maritime House
Basin Road North, Hove
BN41 1WR

Published in Australia
Crabtree Publishing
3 Charles Street
Coburg North
VIC 3058

Contents

Since learning that he has HIV, the virus that can cause AIDS, Magic Johnson has been a public advocate for people with HIV/AIDS. He has lent his name, popularity, and image to support programs and causes in the fight against AIDS. Shown here: souvenir coffee mugs for a fund-raising walk held yearly in Milwaukee to raise money, and increase awareness and support, for people with HIV and AIDS. Magic was the honorary chair of the 1993 walk, which was held nearly two years after he announced to the world that he had tested positive for HIV.

Chapter 1
Magic Man

Magic Johnson in the mid-to late 1980s, at the height of his career with the Los Angeles Lakers.

In the fall of 1974, rumors about a dominant young basketball player spread through the city of Lansing, Michigan. The second-year student at local Everett High School was 15-year-old Earvin Johnson Jr. He had played so well as a freshman that he had led the historically bottom-of-the-barrel Everett Vikings—who rarely won a game—to the state quarterfinals! Now a sophomore, this extraordinary young player was the talk of the town—even the media started paying attention.

A Kid Named Magic

A sports reporter for the local newspaper, the *Lansing State Journal*, heard the rumors about the teenage sensation and attended the Vikings' first game of the 1974–1975 season. After the game, the writer Fred Stabley Jr. said he thought Earvin was "nothing special." He said the teen looked like a solid junior high player, and with a bit of practice, might become "a good high school player one day."

That day came sooner than Fred could have guessed. At the Vikings' next game, he watched in awe as 15-year-old Earvin scored 36 points, grabbed 20 rebounds, and racked up 15 assists and 10 steals.

"People sat there with their mouths open," Fred said later. "They couldn't believe it. It stunned me too. I had never seen anything like this kid at this age."

After the game, Fred headed to the team's locker room to interview Earvin. On his way there, he decided the kid was so good that he needed a fancy nickname. Fred ran through some options in his head. Dr. J was already taken—that was pro player Julius Erving's handle. What about The Big E? Nope. That was Elvin Hayes, another professional b-ball star.

"When I got to his locker," said Fred, "he had this little entourage of junior varsity kids around him, so I waited." As he stood there, the reporter came up with the perfect nickname for the teen.

Finally, it was Fred's turn to talk to Earvin. "We've got to call you something," he said to the young player. "How about Magic?"

Earvin was embarrassed by the attention from the newspaper reporter. "Fine," said Earvin. "Whatever you like." He just wanted the man to leave him to the post-game celebration with his friends—and he certainly didn't take Fred's nickname idea seriously. "I didn't expect to hear that name again, and for a few weeks I didn't," said Earvin.

It turned out that, later that day, Fred's colleagues talked him out of giving the teenager a "hokey" name that he probably couldn't live up to.

It wasn't long, though, before Fred witnessed another spellbinding performance by this astounding young player. At that point, he knew Earvin deserved to be called "Magic." Fred used the nickname in his next article.

"Within about two months, that name was known all across Michigan," said Earvin, who has been known as Magic ever since.

Hoop Dreams

In 1891, students at what is now Springfield College in Springfield, Massachusetts, needed an indoor sport to keep them active during winter months. School leaders asked the physical education teacher, a Canadian named James Naismith, to come up with such a game. They insisted it be a low-contact sport, with low risk for injury to players.

A sculpture showing James Naismith, the inventor of the game of basketball, seated with a soccer ball and peach basket. These were the two main components of the sport back when he invented the game in 1891. The sculpture is in Almonte, Ontario, the Canadian town in which James was born.

After analyzing other sports of the day, James realized that a large ball moves more slowly than a small ball—meaning a player is less likely to get hurt when hit with a large ball. He also found that most injuries happen when players are jostling to score points in front of a ground-level goal line or net. James put those two thoughts together, and came up with basketball—using a soccer ball and a pair of peach baskets nailed high overhead!

The first basketball game in history was played on December 21, 1891, at the college where James worked. Every time a player scored, someone had to climb a ladder to retrieve the ball from the basket. Pretty quickly, the players figured out that, if they cut a hole in the bottom of the basket, they wouldn't have to stop the game every time somebody scored!

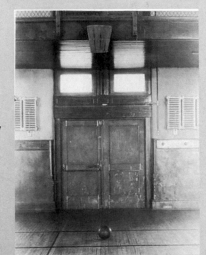

The first basketball court at Springfield College, around the time when the first game was played in 1891. The first "hoop," a peach basket, hangs high above the court.

And the fears about the name being too much for a kid to live up to? Not a problem. Magic's abilities were so astonishing that they appeared almost supernatural. He was an on-court magician.

For the rest of his high school career, and through college, Magic continued to rule the court. He was such a stellar player that he was on the radar of the National Basketball Association (NBA) by the end of his first year in college.

When Magic was ready for the pros the following year, the Los Angeles Lakers nabbed him.

For the next 11 seasons, Magic Johnson dazzled fans as point guard for the Lakers. He was known for his bright smile, brilliant on-court skills, and genuine love for the game of basketball.

With the Lakers, Magic won five NBA championships and six most valuable player (MVP) awards. He was chosen for 12 All-Star teams, and he set record after record for most assists and most steals

In good times and tough times, as a kid, a young man, and later in his life, and on and off the court, Magic Johnson has long been known and loved for his irresistible smile. Top: Magic shares a laugh with singer Paula Abdul at a tribute in his honor at the 2004 NBA All-Star Game. Bottom: Magic flashes his smile during the 1980 NBA Finals vs. the Philadelphia 76ers, which the Lakers won, four games to two. Capping a stellar first season in the NBA, Magic became the first rookie to win the NBA Finals Most Valuable Player (MVP) award.

HOOPS HEAVEN

The Naismith Memorial Basketball Hall of Fame is located in Springfield, Massachusetts, the town that hosted the first basketball game in history.

Being inducted into the Hall of Fame is considered one of basketball's highest honors. Magic Johnson is one of more than 360 players, coaches, teams, and referees to be honored there.

The Hall of Fame was founded in 1959, and opened to the public in 1968. It is now a thriving museum of basketball history.

during regular season play. The term "triple-double" was coined for Magic's uncanny ability to rack up double-digit points, double-digit numbers of rebounds, and double-digit numbers of assists in a single game.

In the 1980s, Magic, among others, led the Lakers through the team's glamorous glory days, known as "Showtime." It was an electrifying era that charged up the Lakers, the NBA, and the nation's love of the game.

TAKING THE GAME NATIONAL

The first "national" professional men's basketball organization in the United States was founded in 1925—but it wasn't exactly a cross-country association. The American Basketball League (ABL) started with nine teams from the East and Midwest. By the end of the 1930–1931 season, only five teams remained, so the league disbanded during the Great Depression.

Two years later, the league started up again, this time with only East Coast cities on the roster. The ABL played its last season of basketball in 1952–1953, existed "on paper" only in 1953–1954, and disbanded permanently in 1955.

Meanwhile, in 1937, another "national" professional basketball association was born. The National Basketball League (NBL) was made up of 13 teams from small cities and towns in the Great Lakes area. Nine years later, in 1946, another pro organization, the Basketball Association

of America (BAA), made its debut with 11 teams, including the Boston Celtics. BAA teams hailed from large cities in the Eastern United States, with one Canadian team based in Toronto.

In 1949, after three years of fighting for teams and players, the NBL and the BAA merged into the National Basketball Association (NBA).

In 1967, the NBA squared off against another newly formed major league-level basketball league, the American Basketball Association (ABA). In 1976, after competing intensely for cities in which to locate teams as well as for top players from the college and pro ranks alike, the two leagues merged under the banner of the NBA. Four teams that had started in the ABA—the New York (later New Jersey and today Brooklyn) Nets, Denver Nuggets, Indiana Pacers, and San Antonio Spurs—joined the NBA and are with the older league to this day.

Today, with 30 teams, the NBA is the main professional basketball organization in North America.

When One Door Closes …

The era known as Showtime was Magic Johnson's heyday. It marked the height of his basketball success, the peak of his fame, and the realization of his childhood dream. Suddenly, though, it all came to a crashing halt. In 1991, Magic received a devastating medical diagnosis—one that required more than magical spells for the hoops superstar to survive.

That fall, he tested positive for HIV (human immunodeficiency virus), the virus that can cause AIDS. At that time, an HIV diagnosis was considered a death sentence. Immediately, the celebrated point guard retired from the NBA to focus on his health. He used his fame to raise awareness, money, and understanding about HIV and AIDS.

He took his medications, lived well, maintained a positive attitude—and today, more than two decades after his diagnosis, Magic continues to thrive. He is living proof that HIV-positive status is not necessarily fatal.

Magic Johnson speaks to a group of students at Walton High School, Bronx, New York City, in March 1992 about the need to practice safe sex, stay in school, and "dream big." Only a few months after announcing to the world that he had tested positive for HIV, the virus that can cause AIDS, Magic was taking his message about HIV/AIDS prevention and care to millions. As a new "face" of a condition that most people preferred to not speak about, Magic helped raise awareness, money, and guidance in the battle against HIV and AIDS. And in the process, he helped give people with HIV and AIDS a new measure of respect, sympathy—and hope.

> *"Although it may seem callous to say so, millions of Americans are lucky that Magic Johnson was infected with HIV. There is no way of calculating how many lives he has saved. No advertising agency could have invented a better, or more effective, role model."*
>
> *The New Yorker,* May 14, 2014

Despite his diagnosis, Magic continued to play basketball on and off until the early years of the 21st century. He has been inducted into the Naismith Memorial Basketball Hall of Fame twice—once for his individual career (2002), and once for playing on the United States 1992 Olympic gold medal-winning "Dream Team" (2010).

In 2010, Magic played on another Dream Team, this one created by President Barack Obama. As part of his 49th birthday celebrations, the president organized an all-star exhibition game for injured members of the military. The president's pick-up game included 15 current and former NBA and college stars.

In 2014, Magic became the second person to receive *Sports Illustrated* magazine's Legacy Award. It is given out, very rarely, "to individuals whose dedication to the ideals of sportsmanship has spanned decades and whose lifetime of achievement in athletics has

> *"[Magic Johnson was] the greatest point guard in NBA history. Magic had [unmatched] vision; he could see players get open and deliver the ball before they even realized they were open. He could play any spot on the court as well."*
>
> J.A. Adande, ESPN sports reporter

… changed the world." Two years later, sports network ESPN named him the number-one point guard in NBA history.

Today, as a respected activist, educator, and fund-raiser, Earvin Johnson Jr. is living another of his childhood dreams. Before he decided to be a basketball player, and when he was still known in the neighborhood as "Junior," his goal was to be a wealthy businessperson.

In 1987, while he was still playing for the Lakers, he founded Magic Johnson Enterprises. The company, which owns real estate, investment, and insurance businesses, along with retail, media, and restaurant operations, is now a billion-dollar organization.

In addition to running his business, raising awareness about HIV/AIDS, and playing the occasional basketball game, Magic also works with youth in at-risk neighborhoods. He provides scholarships and encourages kids to stay in school and to follow their dreams. After all, he was once just like them—a kid from a working-class family with dreams in his heart and stars in his eyes.

If You're Dabbling In Drugs... You Could Be Dabbling With Your Life.

Skin popping, on occasion, seems a lot safer than mainlining. Right? You ask yourself: What can happen? Well, a lot can happen. That's because there's a new game in town. It's called AIDS. So far there are no winners. If you share needles, you're at risk. All it takes is one exposure to the AIDS virus and you've just dabbled your life away.

For more information about AIDS, call 1-800-342-AIDS.

AMERICA RESPONDS TO AIDS

A poster distributed by the Centers for Disease Control and Prevention (CDC), the leading American. national public health institute. The poster was noteworthy in its day (late 1980s–early 1990s) for its use of an image of a young man who did not fit common stereotypes of people who were susceptible to HIV and AIDS. By showing a person who seemed more suited to a message about sports, physical fitness, or some other healthy activity, the CDC sought to drive home the idea that even the most casual "dabbling" in drugs that might involve sharing needles can ruin a young person's life. When Magic Johnson announced that he was HIV-positive, he took that message a step further as a true-to-life example of a person who fit none of the typical images of someone who could get HIV. Magic used his own diagnosis to create an awareness of HIV and AIDS that extended into the mainstream of American life.

HIV and AIDS—A Primer

HIV, which stands for human immunodeficiency virus, is thought to have originated in Africa. Scientists have identified a type of chimpanzee that was the source of HIV. It is believed that the chimpanzee version of the virus, called SIV (simian immunodeficiency virus), was transferred to humans and mutated, or changed, into HIV as far back as the late 1800s. Back then, humans hunted chimps for meat and came into contact with their infected blood.

Over the years, the virus spread across Africa and to other parts of the world. Scientists believe that HIV and AIDS have been in the United States since at least the mid-to late 1970s.

HIV attacks the body's immune system. Our immune systems prevent us from becoming sick and help fight illness when we do get sick. HIV can make the body more susceptible to certain infections. These infections can lead to the condition called AIDS (acquired immunodeficiency syndrome). AIDS comes during the advanced stages of HIV, and as it progresses, the patient cannot fight illnesses, and eventually can die from them.

HIV can be transmitted—passed on from person to person—by body fluids, such as blood, breast milk, and liquids from male and female sex organs. This is why such unsafe practices such as sharing needles and having unprotected sex, especially with multiple partners, can spread HIV from person to person. Some body fluids, such as feces (poop), vomit, saliva, sweat, tears, mucus, and urine, have not been found to transmit HIV, unless they contain infected blood and come into contact with open sores.

Because unborn babies share their mothers' blood, children can be born with HIV. In the past, people receiving blood transfusions (blood donated by others) during medical procedures were at risk of becoming infected by the blood of a donor with HIV. Today, all blood donors are tested for HIV. This has virtually eliminated the risk of receiving HIV-infected blood through transfusions.

Unlike some viruses, HIV is not one that the human body can get rid of entirely, so a person infected with HIV can never be cured. Today, however, HIV can be managed with a combination of medications. The goal is to prevent it from advancing to become AIDS. So a diagnosis of HIV does not mean that a person cannot live a long life. Just ask Magic Johnson!

Chapter 2
Born to Play B-Ball

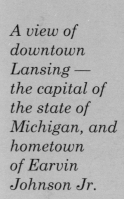

On August 14, 1959, Earvin Johnson and his wife Christine welcomed a bouncing baby boy into the world. The child, named Earvin Johnson Jr., was child number four for the family. To avoid confusion between Earvin Sr. and Earvin Jr., the little boy was known as "Junior." Within three years, the Johnsons added three more babies to the household. In addition to these seven kids were three more from Earvin Sr.'s previous marriage, who also stayed at the Johnson home now and then. "The place turned into a real madhouse before school every morning, when we all lined up to use the one bathroom," remembered Junior. Despite the chaos, it was a close-knit, loving family—and Junior was a happy, smiling child.

A view of downtown Lansing — the capital of the state of Michigan, and hometown of Earvin Johnson Jr.

One Big Happy Family

The Johnson family lived in a working-class, African-American neighborhood in Lansing, Michigan. There, Earvin Sr. worked at General Motors as a welder on an assembly line. Because he worked the night shift, he always had a second, daytime job to earn extra money. Eventually, Earvin bought a truck to run his own trash-

The Michigan State Capitol in Lansing.

hauling business—but he continued to work at GM at night.

On top of caring for a houseful of children, Christine worked outside the home, too—first as a school custodian, and later in a cafeteria.

The family was comfortable, but not wealthy. "We always had enough to eat, but there were plenty of things I wanted and just couldn't have, like a ten-speed bike or blue jeans," said Junior. For a treat, the family would go to movies together and share popcorn, soft drinks, and candy. Sometimes, mom and dad splurged and bought a record, so the family could have music in the house.

Junior's parents were strict and had high expectations. They worked hard and demanded their kids work equally hard. All the children helped around the house, doing dishes, cleaning, and

babysitting their younger siblings. Junior and his brothers also worked outside the home, helping their dad with his hauling business on the weekends.

Said Junior of those days:

"Dad didn't believe in handouts. So as a kid, the only way I could get my hands on any spending money was to go out and earn it. By the time I was ten, I had my own little neighborhood business. I raked leaves, cleaned yards, and shoveled snow."

Religion was important to the Johnsons, especially to Christine. Every Sunday, the whole family attended the local Baptist church, where Junior and his dad sang in the choir. When Junior was about ten years old, though, his mother switched churches. She became a Seventh-day Adventist, which meant she now went to church on Saturdays. This caused a short "war" between Earvin

Earvin Johnson Jr.'s parents, Christine and Earvin Sr., at their home in Lansing, Michigan.

ONE FAMILY, TWO CHURCHES

Christine Johnson became a Seventh-day Adventist in the late 1960s. The Seventh-day Adventist Church is a Christian faith that began in the United States in the mid-1800s. Rather than observe the Sabbath on Sunday, the Seventh-day Adventist Church honors it on Saturday, the seventh day of the week in the Jewish and Christian calendars. By observing the Sabbath between Friday sunset and Saturday sunset, the Church returned to the custom of some early Christians who followed Jewish practice. Seventh-day Adventists follow certain rules about food they can eat, and do not drink alcohol or smoke. They also do not believe in hell as do other Christians.

James and Ellen White, two of the founders of the Seventh-day Adventist Church.

and Christine—they each wanted the other to switch churches. Finally, they agreed to attend different churches. After that, Christine and the girls joined the Adventist church, attending Saturday services, while Earvin and the boys continued on at the Baptist church on Sundays. "My parents loved each other and they fixed things up," said Junior.

Christine was a loving, kind woman with a big, wide smile. "She just [lit] up every place she [went]," said Junior, who inherited his mother's beaming grin. "Mom [got] along with everybody, and she was every kid's mother in our neighborhood."

As much as Junior loved his mom, he was particularly close to his father. "He was my idol."

Earvin Sr. loved basketball. He had played in his youth, and he passed on his passion for the game to his son. "My dad and I had a special bond that continues to this day, and there's no question that basketball made us especially close," said Junior.

On Sunday afternoons, father and son sat side by side in the living room, watching basketball on TV. When Earvin had bits of free time, he and Junior played one-on-one matches

MAGIC MOMENT

Junior Johnson had basketball in his blood. His father had played basketball on his high school team in Mississippi. His mother had also played as a child, as did her brothers. One of Magic's sisters later attended the University of South Carolina on a basketball scholarship.

> *"Physically, I'm not the most gifted basketball player in the world. I've never been the fastest runner or the highest jumper. But thanks to my father, nobody will ever outsmart me on the court."*
>
> Earvin "Magic" Johnson,
> *My Life*, 1992

on the street or on neighborhood courts. Over the years, Earvin taught Junior everything he needed to know about the game he loved. "He taught me to win against the odds, and never to quit."

A Boy and His Basketball

Earvin Johnson Sr. gave his son a basketball when the boy was a preschooler. By the time Junior was six years old, the ball was his constant companion. He even slept with it!

Junior dribbled that ball to school, to the store, and everywhere else he went. Day and night, he practiced his dribbling skills:

> *"I'd run around the parked cars and pretend they were players on the other team, people used to open their windows and yell at me for waking them up. But I couldn't help it. The game was just in me."*

Junior's mother drew the line at dribbling the ball and shooting baskets in the house. Instead, Junior balled up socks and quietly

BOYHOOD B-BALL HEROES

When he was a kid, Earvin Johnson Jr.'s favorite NBA player was Wilt Chamberlain. He also loved Dave Bing, Walt Frazier, Earl Monroe, and Bill Russell. Magic also idolized Kareem Abdul-Jabbar, who became his teammate when Magic was drafted by the Los Angeles Lakers in 1979.

dunked them into laundry baskets and garbage cans. "I wanted to be good, so I practiced and played constantly," he said.

Sometimes, when he was alone on a basketball court, Junior pretended he was playing both sides of an NBA game. His favorite players were Wilt Chamberlain, who then played for the Philadelphia 76ers, and Dave Bing of the Detroit Pistons. "I'd be Chamberlain going one way [on the court] and Bing going the other." He also played the part of the announcer, giving a play-by-play of the action to an imaginary crowd.

"No matter what else I was doing, I always had a basketball in my hand. If I was running an errand for my mother, I'd dribble on the way to the store. Just to make it interesting, I'd alternate right hand and left, block by block."

Earvin "Magic" Johnson,
My Life, 1992

MAGIC'S BOYHOOD B-BALL HERO: WILT CHAMBERLAIN

Born in Philadelphia, Wilt "The Stilt" Chamberlain got his start in professional basketball in 1959 with the Harlem Globetrotters—a team that is famed and beloved worldwide for its incredible blend of athletic skill, theater, and comedy on the basketball court. After a year with the Globetrotters, Wilt began his NBA career with the Philadelphia Warriors. During his time with the Warriors, the team moved to California to become the San Francisco (today Golden State) Warriors. In 1965, he was traded to the Philadelphia 76ers, the team that had taken the Warriors' place in Philly. In 1968, he was traded to the Los Angeles Lakers, where he spent the rest of his professional career. Wilt retired from the NBA in 1973.

The seven-foot-one-inch (216-cm) center is considered one of the greatest basketball players of all time. He is the only player in history to score 100 points in a single game, and to average more than 30 and 40 points in a single season. Throughout his career, he led the league numerous times in scoring, rebounding, and assists, established many all-time NBA records, was a 13-time All-Star, won the league's MVP award four times, and won countless other individual honors. The Globetrotters and all three of his NBA teams retired his jersey (number 13). Wilt died of heart trouble in 1999 at the age of 63.

Wilt Chamberlain in 1959, in his first year of professional basketball, with the Harlem Globetrotters.

When Junior's older brother Larry played with him, Larry pretended he was Walt Frazier of the New York Knicks, another favorite.

Rain or shine, Junior played ball. "By fourth grade I was even going on winter mornings," he said. "Snow wouldn't stop me—I brought a shovel."

In the spring, Junior always had lots of other kids to play with. They played in the schoolyard so much that they wore the lines off the pavement and shredded the basketball net. "The best ball came on late summer afternoons," remembered Junior. "Sometimes we'd be going so well that our older brothers would drive up and flick on the headlights. Then we would play into the night."

The first time Junior played on a real basketball team was when he was in the fifth grade. The sixth graders had just formed their own team, "and the fifth-grade boys were jealous." The kids persuaded Jim Dart, the husband of one of their teachers, to supervise their practice time.

Jim and his wife Greta became Junior's first white friends. "Getting to know the Darts allowed me to start feeling comfortable

Jim and Greta Dart played an important part in Junior's young life. Greta taught Junior in the fifth grade, around the same time that Jim helped Junior and his friends organize their own basketball team. The couple served as role models for the young boy and gave him work to earn money when he wasn't helping out in his dad's business. They also helped nurture Junior in his growing love for basketball.

Magic's Boyhood B-Ball Heroes: Walt Frazier and Earl Monroe

Born in Atlanta, Georgia, Walter "Clyde" Frazier Jr was selected by the New York Knicks in the 1967 NBA draft. While with the Knicks, he picked up the nickname "Clyde" because he wore a hat similar to the one worn by Warren Beatty in the hit 1967 movie *Bonnie and Clyde*. Walt quickly became a star on and off the court. On-court, he was a fast, cool-headed, elegant point guard who led the Knicks to their only NBA championships, in 1970 and 1973. He was named to the NBA All-Star team seven times, winning the All-Star MVP award twice. Off-court, he was known for his colorful clothing, fancy cars, and after-hours partying. Because of his chill personality, Walt was featured in many magazine articles and advertisements, and he was the first NBA player to have a shoe named after him (the "CLYDE," by PUMA). After ten years, the Knicks traded Walt to the Cleveland Cavaliers. He retired two years later. In 1979, the Knicks retired his jersey (number 10). In 2012 he was honored with a place in New York City's Ride of Fame, which honors public figures for having presented New York City in a positive light, and had a double-decker NYC tour bus dedicated to him. Today, he is a sportscaster for the Knicks.

Born in Philadelphia, Pennsylvania, Earl "The Pearl" Monroe was selected by the Baltimore Bullets in the 1967 draft. He spent 14 seasons with the NBA, from 1967 to 1971 with the Bullets (today's Washington Wizards), and from 1971 to 1980 with the New York Knicks. In New York, he played alongside Walt Frazier. The duo became known as "the Rolls Royce Backcourt"—one of the most effective guard pairings in history. The 1968 NBA Rookie

Walt "Clyde" Frazier (number 10) and Earl "The Pearl" Monroe (number 15) flank their head coach, Red Holzman, in this detail from a team photo of the 1975 New York Knicks.

of the Year and a four-time NBA All-Star, Earl was known for his flashy style of play and on-court success, which led to his nickname Earl "The Pearl." He retired from the NBA in 1980 because of knee and leg injuries. Since then, he has created a record company, managed musicians, opened and closed restaurants, helped promote diabetes-friendly eating and heart health, worked as a sports commentator, and launched a successful candy company. His jersey has been retired by both the Knicks (number 15) and the Washington Wizards (number 10).

SPEECHLESS IN DETROIT

In 1971, when he was 11 years old, Junior met one of his idols. He and a group of kids from the local Boys Club went to Detroit to watch the Pistons play the Milwaukee Bucks. After the game, some of the boys were invited to the Milwaukee locker room. Junior desperately wanted to ask superstar player Lew Alcindor for his autograph.

"Suddenly, there he was, standing right in front of me. But I was so nervous that I couldn't even open my mouth. Another kid had to ask him for me."

Lew signed but didn't say anything to the youth. "He wasn't very friendly about it," remembered Junior.

Little did the boy know that the famous player would one day be his teammate!

Oh, and a few months after this meeting, Lew changed his name to Kareem Abdul-Jabbar.

Kareem Abdul-Jabbar with the Milwaukee Bucks in 1971, when he was still known as Lew Alcindor. The hook shot in this photo became a "trademark" Kareem shot—the skyhook.

with white people." The husband and wife also ended up becoming role models and second parents to Junior.

When Earvin Sr. didn't need his help with the hauling business, Junior worked for the Darts, doing yard work and maintenance on rental homes they owned. Jim also took Junior to watch nearby high school and college games. One summer, he paid for Junior to attend a basketball camp at nearby Michigan State University.

By the time Junior entered grade seven at Dwight Rich Junior High, he was six feet (cm) tall and ready to try out for the school basketball team. About 100 kids showed up to the first try-out—but the coach only needed 12 players.

Immediately, he asked the right-handed kids to dribble and shoot a basket with their left hands, and the lefties to dribble and shoot with their right. "Most kids just couldn't do it, and the coach cut them on the spot," said Junior. "In about twenty minutes, that gym cleared out and [the coach] had his team. I made the team because Jim Dart had worked with us on our weak-hand shooting, and also because I had practiced so much."

During his junior high years, coaches worked with Junior to help him rely less on his height, and more on his on-court agility and assertiveness. They pushed him to run for rebounds and work on his shooting skills. "By ninth grade our team was unstoppable," said Junior. In one particularly memorable game, he scored an astounding 48 points. (That's almost double what a high-scoring high school player might typically score in a game.)

Up to that point, Earvin Johnson had never seen his son play basketball with the school team—he was always at work at game time. After Junior's 48-pointer, though, the kid was the talk of the town. Earvin Sr. asked his boss for time off so he could watch his son play. The foreman knew all about the local basketball whiz kid, and agreed Earvin should be at Junior's games. "From then on, Dad didn't miss a game," said Junior.

Black and White

By the time he entered high school, Junior Johnson knew he wanted a career as a professional ball player. He certainly had the right build—by this time, he was six-foot-five (196 cm) and still growing!

He couldn't wait to start classes at nearby Sexton High. "It was the pride of the west side [of Lansing], and was known throughout the state of Michigan as a basketball powerhouse," he said. An "all-black school ... five blocks from our house," Sexton was where many of Junior's friends would go.

A year earlier, though, in its efforts to desegregate its school system, the city of Lansing had changed school boundaries. That meant Junior no longer lived in the Sexton area. "Our family lived just outside the cutoff line," he said. "Suddenly we weren't allowed to go to Sexton with all our friends."

Instead, Junior was to be bused to all-white Everett High School. The previous year, his elder siblings Larry and Pearl were in the first group of African-American kids to be bused to Everett. Because their oldest brother Quincy had started high school before the boundary changes, he continued at Sexton. Said Junior:

"I was furious. No black kid wanted to attend an all-white school. But for me, being sent to Everett was an especially cruel punishment. Maybe if Everett had had a great basketball team I could have lived with it. Or even a half-decent team. But the Vikings were terrible."

Lansing school zones were redrawn the year before Junior Johnson began high school. Junior was upset to discover that he would be unable to attend J. W. Sexton High (shown top in a historic photo). Sexton was in Junior's neighborhood and was at that time an all-black school. Instead of Sexton, however, Junior was assigned to Everett High School (shown bottom). A newer school with a nearly all-white student body, Everett was on another side of town. An added minus: At that time, it didn't have Sexton's reputation as a state high school basketball powerhouse. Today, the two schools are strong athletic rivals.

Junior did everything he could to convince the school board to allow him to attend Sexton. He even pretended he had left his family and moved in with friends on the Sexton side of the dividing line.

The school board didn't buy it, and in the fall of 1973, Junior started taking the bus to Everett High School. At the time, about 100 African-American students attended Everett. He later wrote:

> *"We were only the second group of black kids to attend the school. The previous year, a few whites had thrown rocks at the buses. Some white parents had even kept their kids out of school rather than let them attend classes with blacks."*

By the time Junior arrived at Everett, things had settled down a bit. But the two groups still didn't mix.

In Larry's first year at Everett, he had gotten into fights with some of the white kids. He had made the basketball team, but was kicked off after he argued with the coach. Larry asked Junior to stand by him and boycott the basketball team. "I couldn't go along with what he was asking," said Junior. "The idea of playing for Everett sounded horrible to me, no question about it, but not playing sounded even worse."

The 14-year-old easily made the basketball team, but he wasn't easily accepted by his white teammates. At first, nobody would throw the ball to Junior. When he became aggressive, grabbed a rebound, and sunk a basket, the others told him it wasn't his place to score points. One day, Junior almost came to blows with a teammate.

At that point, Coach George Fox stepped in. He asked Junior to be more tolerant of the other boys. "What was he talking about? Why should *I* have to be tolerant?" Junior secretly hoped the near-fight would get him transferred to another school—hopefully Sexton!

That didn't happen. Instead, Coach Fox discussed the black-and-white situation with the rest of the team. After that, the others still gave Junior the silent treatment, but at least they let him play a little more.

Soon, one of the other players took Junior under his wing, and the other boys came eventually around—especially after they

Magic's Boyhood B-Ball Hero: Dave Bing

Born in Washington, D.C., Dave Bing played 12 years in the NBA, mostly with the Detroit Pistons, who selected him in the 1966 draft. After leaving the Pistons in 1975, he also played two years with the Washington Bullets (today the Washington Wizards), followed by a year with the Boston Celtics, before retiring in 1978. As a guard, he was known not only for his playmaking abilities, but also for shooting and scoring. In the 1967–1968 season, Dave was the NBA scoring champion with an average of 27.1 points per game, and during his career he averaged 20.3 points per game. He played in seven NBA All-Star games, winning the All-Star MVP award in 1976. His jersey (number 21) has been retired by the Pistons. After his NBA career, Dave founded a successful steel company and later became mayor of Detroit.

Dave Bing spent most of his 12-year NBA career playing for the Detroit Pistons.

realized just how talented this new kid was.

Because of Junior's outstanding basketball skills, and because of his smiling, friendly personality, the teachers at Everett quickly realized that—unlike his hotheaded brother—Junior had the makings of a leader. During his high school career, they often turned to him to help resolve racial issues at the school.

As much as he had initially hated the idea of going to Everett, Junior later said that being bused to the school was one of the best things

THE NOT-SO-DISTANT PAST

Earvin Johnson Sr. was born in Mississippi. After his father abandoned the family, the youngster spent his days working on a farm to help support his mother and siblings. He rarely had time to go to school.

Christine Johnson grew up on a farm in North Carolina. She and her nine siblings worked the land before and after school.

When Earvin Sr. and Christine were young, racial segregation was very much a part of life in the southern United States. Washrooms, restaurants, buses, and other services were designated for white people only. African Americans often had to use separate entrances and facilities.

Earvin Sr. and Christine moved north to Michigan to find jobs, so they could earn money for their family. Every summer, though, the Johnsons took their kids south to visit relatives. "Even in the early seventies we used to bring our own food on these trips, and we ate our meals in rest areas along the way," said Junior. "It was a lot cheaper that way, but this wasn't the only reason. When you were down South, you never knew when a restaurant would flat out refuse to serve you."

U.S. troops escort African-American students attempting to attend Little Rock Central High School after the governor of Arkansas attempted to block black students from the previously all-white school. This photo was taken in 1957, about two years before Magic Johnson was born.

An African-American man climbs the stairs leading to the "colored" entrance of a movie theater in Mississippi in 1939.

that had ever happened to him. "It got me out of my own little world and taught me how to understand white people, how to communicate and deal with them."

Rising Star

Everett High's basketball coach, George Fox, was a good leader who focused on the fundamentals of the game and on players' individual strengths. He recognized that, even though Junior Johnson was the tallest kid on the team, his skills were best used in the point guard position.

Typically, the tallest players become the centers, the ones who shoot baskets. The point guard is the on-court leader—a good ball handler and passer who also makes decisions and calls plays during a game.

With Junior on the team as point guard, the Everett Vikings—who were used to losing— started winning their games.

In Junior's second season at Everett, word started to circulate about this hot young high school basketball player. Even the media began paying attention. That's when *Lansing State Journal* sports reporter Fred Stabley Jr. began attending Everett's games. He wanted to scope out this new kid to see if he was as good as everyone said.

He was. After one particularly brilliant game, Fred told the 15-year-old whiz kid he needed a nickname. When he made the "Magic" suggestion, "my friends and I bust out laughing," said Junior. "What? Magic? I never thought it would stick."

Before long, the kid who wore number 32

on his uniform was known as Magic Johnson—
and his reputation extended far beyond the
school district. By the end of his second year at
Everett, college teams were already expressing
interest in the magical 15-year-old.

In his senior year of high school, Magic
led his team to a 27–1 win-loss record and to
the state finals, where the Vikings won the
championship game in overtime. By then,
dozens of colleges were hard-core courting the
basketball superstar, offering scholarships,
flying him across the country to tour their
schools, and sending his mom flowers.

"There were so many calls that we had to
change our phone number," remembered Magic.
After much thought, he narrowed the field to
two schools that were both in Michigan.

Everyone in Lansing had an opinion about
which school Magic should choose. College
recruiters, coaches, his family, even the media
anxiously awaited his decision.

For Magic, it was a tough call. Should he do
the logical thing and choose the college with
the better academic programs and superior
basketball team? Or should he follow his heart
and go with the school whose basketball squad
he considered his home team?

MAGIC'S BOYHOOD B-BALL HERO: BILL RUSSELL

Born in West Monroe, Louisiana, Bill Russell was selected by the St. Louis (now Atlanta) Hawks in the 1956 draft and traded to the Boston Celtics before the season began. The lanky center played his entire 13-year professional career with the Celtics, with whom he won 11 NBA championships. That's a record for an athlete in any major North American sports league. (Tied for the record is former hockey player Henri Richard, who won 11 Stanley Cups with the National Hockey League Montreal Canadiens.)

Bill was also a four-time NBA rebounding leader, 12-time All-Star, winner of the All-Star MVP in 1963, and five-time NBA MVP. In his first NBA season (1956–1957), he became the first player in NBA history to average more than 20 rebounds a game, and he is considered to have set new standards for excellence in rebounding and defensive play generally throughout his career. During his final three years with the Celtics (1966–1969), he also served as the team's head coach. This made him the first-ever African American to coach in the NBA, and the first black head coach in any major North American professional sports league.

The Celtics won the championship in two of Bill's three years as a player-coach. Several years after retiring in 1969, he returned to coaching in two

stints—with the Seattle SuperSonics in 1973–1977, and the Sacramento Kings in 1987–1988. Off the court, he tried his hand at sports commentating, some business pursuits, and writing several books.

But none of these things brought him the same amount of success he had achieved on the basketball court, for which he has received recognition and awards that are too numerous to list here. In 1972, the Celtics retired his jersey (number 6), and in 2009 the NBA announced that its NBA Finals MVP award would be renamed the Bill Russell NBA Finals Most Valuable Player Award. Considered one of the greatest players in NBA history, Bill was named "Sportsman of the Year" by *Sports Illustrated* in 1968, "Athlete of the Decade" by *The Sporting News* in 1970, and "Greatest Player in the History of the NBA" by the Professional Basketball Writers Association of America in 1980.

Throughout his career and in his post-playing years, Bill has been an outspoken and sometimes controversial champion of human rights and equality. During the height of his basketball career, he was an active member of the civil rights movement. In 1963, he went to Mississippi during a time of great racial tension to help register black voters and set up a racially integrated basketball camp. He also marched in civil rights rallies, including the 1963 March on Washington, where he stood near Martin Luther King Jr. as the inspirational leader delivered his historic "I Have a Dream" speech. For these and other social endeavors, as well as his impact on the game of basketball, Bill was awarded the Presidential Medal of Freedom by President Barack Obama in 2011.

Three images from the life and times of basketball great and champion of human rights, Bill Russell. Left: in 1956 with head coach Red Auerbach in his first year playing for the Boston Celtics. Middle: as a participant (hatless at left) in the 1963 March on Washington for human rights, at which Martin Luther King Jr. delivered his famous "I Have a Dream" speech. Right: in the Green Room of the White House with President Barack Obama and First Lady Michelle Obama, waiting to receive the 2011 Presidential Medal of Freedom for his accomplishments in sports and his work in civil rights.

Chapter 3
King of the College Court

On April 22, 1977, 18-year-old Magic Johnson held a press conference attended by reporters from all over the country. His choice of college was such a big sports story that his announcement was broadcast live on radio. When the celebrated teenager stepped up to the microphone, nobody but his parents and future coach knew what he was about to say. Most people expected he would choose the University of Michigan—in Ann Arbor over Michigan State University in neighboring East Lansing. Both colleges were members of the powerhouse Big Ten Conference, but the University of Michigan had the stronger basketball team. Magic surprised them all. "I have decided to attend Michigan State University," he announced to cheers and applause from his hometown audience. "I was born to be a Spartan."

Michigan is home to two Big Ten universities, each of them a possible destination for Magic Johnson after his graduation from high school in 1977. Left: Beaumont Tower, which marks the site of the first building on the campus of Michigan State University in nearby East Lansing. Right: the Michigan Union building, home of most student groups at the University of Michigan in Ann Arbor.

> *"I really liked the idea of ... going with the underdog and trying to bring them into the upper echelon. That's what had happened at Everett. We had won the high school title with a team that nobody took seriously. My goal was to do the same thing in college."*
>
> Magic Johnson, on why he chose Michigan State University

Spartan Magic

In choosing Michigan State, Magic had decided to stay close to family and friends in Lansing and play for the team he had grown up watching.

The school was just a ten-minute drive from home, but the young man chose to live on campus. He wanted to immerse himself in the college experience and meet new people. He majored in telecommunications with a minor in education. He also worked as a deejay ("E.J. the deejay") at a local disco.

Mostly, though, Magic Johnson played basketball.

In the 1976–1977 season—the one before Magic joined Michigan State—the Spartans had logged a disappointing 10–17 overall record, and their 7–11 record in the Big Ten landed them fifth in the conference. When Magic joined the team, Michigan State hadn't made it to a national tournament since the 1958–1959 season.

One of the reasons Magic chose to join the Spartans was because he knew he could help the "hometown team" win. The other reason was because Spartans coach Jud Heathcote had promised Magic that he could play point guard.

Most university coaches who had tried to recruit Magic had pegged the six-foot-nine-inch (206-cm) player as a center. But Jud offered to let Magic lead the team as point guard. It was what Magic wanted—but it was a lot of pressure on a young player.

In his first game as a Spartan, Magic said he "stunk up the gym" with a "turkey" of a performance. "All my family and friends were there to see my debut. But with so much advance press and all those expectations, I was just too fired up to play well."

Still, the Spartans managed to win that game—and they kept on winning.

Because of Magic's reputation, and because the team was finally flourishing, fans came to games by the thousands. Before long, they also began flooding into the gym to watch the Spartans' practices. "It seemed like everyone on campus was a basketball fan," said Magic.

Eventually, coach Heathcote had to ban spectators from practices because the team couldn't get any work done.

In his first year with Michigan State, Magic helped turn the team around. The Spartans finished the 1977–1978 season with a 25–5 overall record, and were 15–3 in league play against other Big Ten teams. They also won the Big Ten conference title, and moved on to the National Collegiate

MAGIC MOMENT

In high school, Magic wore number 32 on his jersey. When he moved to the Spartans, that number was already taken, so he chose number 33 instead.

A New Playing Field

Magic had to make some adjustments in his shift from high school to college basketball.

In high school, he had been the sole dominant player in the league. In college, he found that every team had at least two or three top-notch players who could challenge him. "The college game was also more physical," he said. "These guys were big and strong, and the referees allowed plenty of banging and bruising. It took me about a year to get used to it."

Magic also had to come up with a plan to lead the Spartans to victory. In the past, he had often played "with no real plan in mind." That didn't work at this level.

"The biggest adjustment of all was the quality and intensity of the play." He credits coach Jud Heathcote—gruff on the outside, with a heart of gold on the inside—with helping him make the move to becoming a better player.

Athletic Association (NCAA) championship tournament. There, the Spartans got as far as the regional finals, known as the Elite Eight. Unfortunately for the team and its fans, they lost that round to the University of Kentucky Wildcats—the team that went on to win the championship that year.

Still, 1977–1978 was a stellar year for this historically weak squad. Magic had expected the Spartans to do well under his leadership, but even he was surprised by the well magical, turnaround. "I didn't expect anything like what happened," he said.

By the end of Magic's freshman year with

Michigan State, he was already on the NBA's radar. While he was grateful for the attention, he felt he wasn't ready to turn pro yet.

He wanted to take the Spartans to the top:

"It was nice to be considered, but I knew in my heart that I wasn't ready for the NBA, either physically or mentally. There would be time for that, but right now I wanted at least one more season at Michigan State."

In the Spotlight

In Magic Johnson's second year at Michigan State, his star continued to rise.

In the fall of 1978, the 19-year-old made the cover of *Sports Illustrated* magazine. The publication had named him one of the top-ten sophomore college basketball players in the country. "Within weeks, I went from being known throughout Michigan to being recognized all over the country," said Magic. "Fans started lining up for autographs—I must have signed thousands of that cover alone."

On the inside pages of the magazine was a profile of Magic titled "He's Gone to the Head of His Class." To see Magic play was to watch him, in the words of the article's author, Larry Keith,

"... gliding down [the] court, weaving in and out of traffic, frustrating his defensive man, checking the left and right lanes, waiting, waiting, waiting until just the right moment, and then—presto!—there it is, around his back, through his legs, side-arm, overhand, whatever sleight of hand it takes to get the ball to the right man in the right place at the right time."

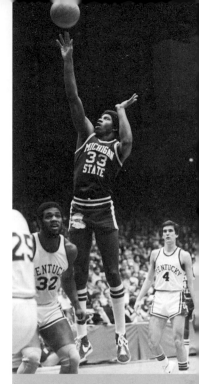

Magic Johnson shoots against the University of Kentucky Wildcats during the 1978 NCAA tournament. It was the end of Magic's freshman year, and he had already begun attracting the attention of NBA scouts.

THE COMPLICATED WORLD
OF COLLEGE BALL

In the United States, more than 1,000 colleges and universities have basketball teams that play in the National Collegiate Athletic Association (NCAA) system. The NCAA is split into three divisions, depending on the quality of athletic ability, sports budget, and number of athletic scholarships of the schools involved. Division I is the highest-caliber group in the NCAA. Michigan State University, where Magic Johnson played, is one of about 350 schools with basketball teams in Division I.

Division I is further divided into many smaller groupings, most of which are called conferences, leagues, or associations. These are similar to the sports leagues with which we are all familiar on the professional level, such as the NBA. These collegiate conferences are usually, although not always, organized geographically. Michigan State is part of the Big Ten Conference—the oldest Division I conference in the country.

When Magic was in college, there were ten teams in the Big Ten. Despite the name, there are now 14 teams in the conference. It originally consisted primarily of schools in states of the Upper Midwest clustered around the Great Lakes, but it now stretches as far west as Nebraska and as far east as New Jersey.

Each season, teams compete within their conferences. Most teams also play non-conference opponents, usually in the early part of the season, before conference play begins. In men's basketball, the 32 conference champions automatically advance to the NCAA Men's Division 1 Basketball Championship tournament. There, they compete to become National Champion with another 36 teams that are issued what are called at-large bids by a selection committee. (The Women's Division I tournament, which also attracts huge numbers of fans, is organized similarly to the Men's.)

Most of the NCAA tournament takes place over a series of weekends in March and April. It has come to be known as "March Madness," and is one of the most popular sporting events in the country.

The tournament consists of seven rounds of play. As the field narrows, particularly following the opening rounds, interest and excitement build. Winning teams advance to the regional semifinals (known as the Sweet Sixteen), then to the regional finals (the Elite Eight), the national semifinals (the Final Four), and finally the National Finals in which the two remaining teams play for the National Championship.

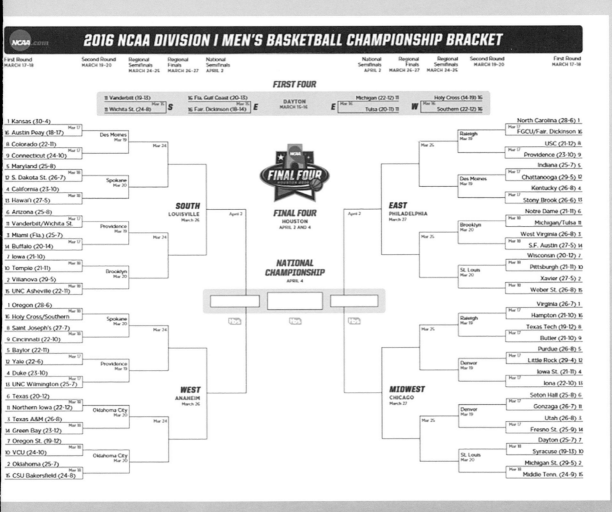

This diagram shows the brackets, or divisions, into which the NCAA Men's Division I Championship tournament was organized in 2016. The brackets are filled in with winning teams as the field narrows toward the center, when the two remaining teams play for the National Championship.

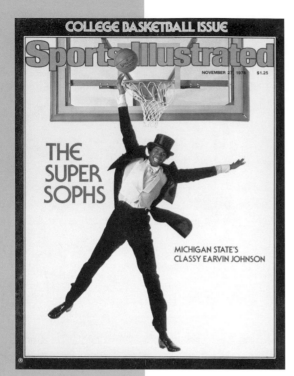

This issue of Sports Illustrated *magazine, in its preview of the 1978–1979 college basketball season, featured Magic on the cover as one of the nation's "Super Sophs."*

He described the teenager as a modest, classy young man, both on and off the court. Magic's b-ball brilliance, he said, was in his ability to read the game, predict what would happen next, and react to it before it happened.

Coach Heathcote agreed that number 33's talent was in "controlling, not dominating" the game. "In Earvin's case, you don't talk about the points he scores," he said, "but the points he produces. Not just the baskets and assists, but the first pass that makes the second pass possible. He's conscious of scoring himself, but it isn't an obsession with him."

A few months after *Sports Illustrated* turned Magic Johnson into a household name, the Associated Press named Michigan State the top college team in the country.

And then the Spartans started losing.

After the team lost four of its next six games, Magic started to wonder if the praise in the *Sports Illustrated* article had jinxed the team.

He and his teammates were so frustrated that they approached the coach as a group and suggested he was holding them back. "Ever since we were ranked number one, Jud had been overcoaching the team," said Magic. "He was slowing us down, not letting us run and gun."

Jud disagreed with his players' assessment, "but what made him a great leader was that he knew how to listen," said Magic.

The coach agreed to try a new approach, one that took the players' concerns into account. With this change in strategy, the Spartans won their next ten games in a row. They finished the season with an overall record of 26–6 and a 13–5 record in the Big Ten, earning them a place in the NCAA playoffs for the second year running.

In their first round of play, the Spartans easily beat Lamar University, 95–64. "Next came Louisiana State," said Magic. "We beat them [87–71] without much trouble."

That Sweet Sixteen win took the Spartans to the regional final, the Elite Eight round, against the University of Notre Dame. "[It] was shaping up to be the biggest battle of the year," said Magic. "They had a history of beating us and we were itching to get even."

The Spartans did just that, beating Notre Dame by 12 points. "When the game was over, we were almost delirious with excitement."

The following weekend, in the Final Four, the Michigan State Spartans played the University of Pennsylvania Quakers. Michigan State played so well that "the game was essentially over by halftime," said Magic. The final score was 101–67, and with that, the Spartans were off to the National Championship game. Their opponents? The Indiana State Sycamores.

Not only was Indiana State undefeated for the entire 1978–1979 season, but it also had a superstar on its roster—a forward named Larry Bird. "We wanted to be the team that finally stopped them," said Magic. "I had another goal: I wanted to be the guy who stopped Larry Bird."

MAGIC MOMENT

Weirdly, and coincidentally, Magic Johnson and Larry Bird both wore number 33 on their jerseys in college.

Michigan State's Magic Johnson and Indiana State's Larry Bird answer reporters' questions before their teams square off in the 1979 NCAA Championship game in Salt Lake City, Utah.

Magic cuts the net as he, his teammates, and their fans celebrate Michigan State's 75–64 win over Indiana State for the 1979 NCAA Men's Division I National Championship.

We Are the Champions

At the time, Magic and Larry were considered the two best college players in the country—and they were about to meet on the court for the first time. Indiana State was favored to win the big game, but Michigan State came prepared.

"The pressure was enormous," said Magic. "Every moment was intense and every play huge. Every move you made, you knew the entire country was watching. Later, we were told that this was the most widely watched game in the history of college basketball."

The Spartans led for most of the contest, but with about ten minutes left to play, their lead tightened to just six points. Could they hold on? Could the Michigan State defense keep Larry Bird caged to the end? Would they make history that day?

The answer was yes! On March 26, 1979, by the time the final buzzer had sounded, the Spartans were on top 75–64. Michigan State University won the NCAA championship for the first time in its history. Magic was named MVP of the Final Four teams.

As he and his teammates celebrated their victory, Magic glanced across the court to see Larry with his face buried in a towel. "He was obviously crying, and my heart went out to him," said Magic. "I knew in my gut that this wasn't the end of the story. Somehow, somewhere, Larry Bird and I would be seeing each other again."

He was right about that. The relationship between the two superstar players was soon to become one of the greatest rivalries in American sports history.

BASKETBALL BIRD

Larry Bird was born in 1956 in the tiny town of West Baden, in the heart of Indiana corn country. He grew up poor, his parents divorced when he was in high school, and his father committed suicide a year later.

Larry was a talented athlete who loved many sports. It wasn't until his final years of high school that he realized pro basketball could be his future. He accepted a scholarship to Indiana University, but quit school after a few weeks. A year later, he enrolled at Indiana State University, where he became a superstar.

Larry Bird playing for the Boston Celtics in 1984–1985, one of his three-in-a-row MVP seasons.

The Boston Celtics drafted Larry at the end of the 1977–1978 season, but the young player deferred the offer for a year. He wanted to earn his college degree before turning pro.

After graduation, and for the following 13 years, Larry played with the Celtics, helping them win three NBA championships. He was also a 12-time NBA All-Star and claimed numerous individual honors, including NBA Rookie of the Year, an All-Star Game MVP award, two NBA Finals MVPs, and three consecutive NBA MVP awards (1984–1986).

After winning an Olympic gold medal as part of the United States "Dream Team" in 1992 (a team that included Magic Johnson), Larry Bird retired from playing professional basketball.

Magic Johnson and Larry Bird line up for a foul shot during the 1979 NCAA National Championship game.

The Celtics retired his jersey (number 33), but Larry has remained involved in the NBA ever since, as a coach and executive. He continued to work for the Celtics from 1992–1997 as a special assistant in their front office. From 1997–2000, he returned to his home state to become head coach of the Indiana Pacers, leading the team to two consecutive Central Division titles and a spot in the 2000 NBA Finals. In 2003, he returned to the Pacers, and other than a one-year break in 2012–2013, he has been with the team as President of Basketball Operations. He has the distinction of being the only person in NBA history to have won the MVP, Coach of the Year, and Executive of the Year awards.

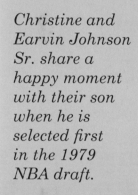

Chapter 4
Believing in Magic

After Magic Johnson's magical sophomore season with the Michigan State Spartans, the NBA came calling again. This time, two teams wanted him—the Los Angeles Lakers and the Chicago Bulls. This time, though, it didn't matter which team Magic preferred. The Lakers had first pick in the college draft—and the Lakers wanted Magic Johnson. The only choice Magic had was whether he would turn pro with the Lakers immediately, or stay in college another year. "It was a very difficult decision," he said. But he had already accomplished everything he had set out to do with the Spartans. He had helped turn the losing team around to win the Big Ten championship one year, and the national title the next. "It was time to go."

Christine and Earvin Johnson Sr. share a happy moment with their son when he is selected first in the 1979 NBA draft.

The Kid Turns Pro

Not everyone thought Magic was ready for the pros.

In the spring of 1979, when the Lakers drafted him, some people thought his skills weren't yet up to NBA standards. Others believed he was too young and tender to survive the tough world of professional basketball—after all, the kid was only 19.

Even the "Lakers' top brass" had reservations about Magic. "They

THE LAKERS OF L.A.

In 1947, a group of businessmen bought the Detroit Gems—a team in the old National Basketball League (NBL). The new owners moved the Gems to Minneapolis, Minnesota. Because the state was known as "the Land of Ten Thousand Lakes," they called the team the Minneapolis Lakers.

In the team's first year, it won the NBL championship. The following season, the team played in a different league, the Basketball Association of America (BAA)—and won that championship title, too.

In 1949, the NBL and BAA merged to form the NBA. The Lakers became the first-ever champs of this new league. Then, after winning three more titles in the next four years, the Lakers fell into a prolonged slump, posting losing records for six years in a row. Audiences shrank to the point that the team couldn't go on—at least not in Minneapolis.

In 1960, the Lakers moved to Los Angeles. Not an instant hit on the West Coast, fan support grew over the years. By 1965, audience numbers had increased enough that club owner Jack Cooke built the team its own arena—the Forum.

Still, it would be 12 years before the L.A. Lakers won their first NBA championship. That finally happened in 1972. The following year, the team lost to the New York Knicks in the NBA Finals—then the losing began in earnest. For the next six years, the Lakers made the Western Conference Finals once (and lost), lost twice in the Western Conference Semifinals, lost once in the first round of the playoffs, and twice failed to make the playoffs at all. Fed-up fans started calling the team the L.A. "Fakers."

Of course, that all changed in the 1979–1980 season, when Magic Johnson joined the team!

The Lakers then and now. Top: A team photo of the 1950 Minneapolis Lakers. Bottom: A detail from a photo of President Barack Obama with the 2010 NBA Champion L.A. Lakers.

worried that I was a flash in the pan, a college showpiece … who wouldn't survive in the pros," he said. "They also wondered about my size. At the time, all the experts agreed that a big man couldn't be an effective point guard."

One person who believed in Magic was the Lakers' new owner Jerry Buss. "He liked my style and enthusiasm and believed that bringing me to Los Angeles would help put fans in the seats." Even though Lakers officials and coaches wanted to select a different player, Jerry insisted they choose Magic—and Jerry was the boss.

At the time, the Lakers' top-paid player, Kareem Abdul-Jabbar, made about $650,000 a year. When Magic began his salary negotiations with the Lakers, he asked for $600,000 a year. If he didn't get his price, he said, he would return to Michigan State and play another year or two. Another NBA team was certain to come calling before long.

The Lakers refused to pay Magic that much—but they also refused to let him walk away. After some back-and-forth bargaining, the two sides agreed to a half-million dollar package that included money, perks, and bonuses.

"When I left Los Angeles [after the negotiations] I was the highest-paid rookie in the history of the NBA," said Magic. "That lasted for about a month. Then the Celtics signed Larry Bird for $600,000."

(Larry had been drafted by the Boston Celtics in 1978, but had deferred the offer for a year so he could finish his college degree.)

In the summer of 1979, Magic said goodbye to his family in Michigan and moved across the country to join the NBA. "The first time I ever saw my dad cry was the day I left Lansing to move to Los Angeles," he said. "Mom was crying, too, of course. I was a wreck."

"Some kids can't wait to leave home and live on their own. But I was just the opposite.... The thought of moving away from my family just tore me up. My father had always been my best friend, and Mom had always been there with that hot meal or that big hug."

Magic Johnson, on moving to L.A. to join the Lakers

Magic and team owner Jerry Buss have a laugh during their wait for a flight out of L.A. during the 1980 NBA playoffs.

Life in Los Angeles was like a dream come true for Magic. He was now a superstar pro basketball player, living in one of the most exciting cities in the world, and earning packs of money. "I was the loneliest guy in town. I should have been the happiest guy on earth," he said. "But for the first few months, I was miserable."

Unlike college, where everyone had been young, single, and struggling to juggle classes and basketball games, Magic's Laker teammates all had lives and families off the court. Plus, they were a tightly knit crew, and he was the new kid trying to break in.

Again, team owner Jerry Buss came to Magic's rescue. He

took the young player under his wing. He helped Magic find a place to live and invited him to his house in the evenings. Jerry was divorced and rich, and he was happy to share his world of parties, celebrities, and glitzy nightlife:

"Jerry used to invite me over to his house where we'd eat chocolate donuts and play pool. He was divorced and he dated the most beautiful women in town. Sometimes we would double-date, going out for dinner or dancing. A couple of times I went with him to Las Vegas…. Some of my teammates were jealous because I was friends with the owner, but Jerry extended the same invitation to everybody on the team. I was the only one who accepted. He did treat me especially well, however."

In the years that followed, the excitement and glamour that went along with being "friends with the owner" would become something of a blueprint for Magic's life in L.A. and the NBA. But for now, Magic was still, in

"One of my first friends in Los Angeles was the new owner, Jerry Buss. We were like a couple of kids, both of us full of energy and new ideas. People thought my enthusiasm wouldn't last, and they said the same about Jerry. But then, he wasn't exactly your typical franchise owner."

Earvin "Magic" Johnson, *My Life*, 1992

THE LEADER OF THE LAKERS

Jerry Buss was born in Salt Lake City, Utah, in 1933. He and his mother moved to Los Angeles when Jerry was nine, then to Wyoming a few years later. After graduating from the University of Wyoming, Jerry returned to Los Angeles to earn a Ph.D. (doctoral degree) in chemistry at the University of Southern California.

Magic Johnson and Jerry Buss at a ceremony in 2006 honoring Jerry with a star on the Hollywood Walk of Fame. After insisting on selecting Magic in the first round of the 1979 NBA draft and offering Magic support during his first year in the league, Jerry remained one of Magic's most cherished friends, right up to the time of Jerry's death at the age of 80 in 2013.

He worked as a chemist for a few years, but soon discovered there was more money to be made in real estate. By the time he was 34, Jerry was a millionaire. A decade later, he purchased the Los Angeles Lakers basketball team, the Los Angeles Kings hockey team, and the Forum, in which the two teams played.

Jerry was known as a playboy—a wealthy ladies' man who surrounded himself with beautiful women, loved to party, and hung out with the stars. Combining his love of Hollywood glitz and glamour with his passion for basketball, Jerry transformed the Lakers from so-so to what would be known in L.A. as "Showtime."

He was considered "a true visionary," and "one of the great innovators that any sport has ever encountered," said former Lakers coach Pat Riley. Jerry is credited with changing the course, and raising the profile, not just of the Lakers but of the entire NBA. When he died of cancer in February 2013, his six children inherited his majority ownership of the Lakers.

his words, "Earvin Johnson, with butterflies in his stomach ... getting ready to play his first season of big-league ball."

Rookie on the Court

From his first day of training camp with the Lakers in 1979, Magic's exuberance and dazzling smile lit up the basketball court.

In November 1979, within weeks of beginning his rookie season in the NBA, Magic once again made the front cover of Sports Illustrated. *This photo shows him at work against the Denver Nuggets in a pre-season exhibition game.*

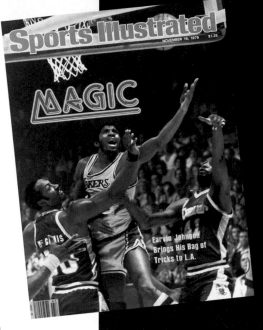

His more experienced teammates thought he would settle down after the initial excitement wore off. "They had seen rookies come and go, and I'm sure they expected that my high spirits would fizzle out within a few weeks," said Magic. Of course it didn't. Magic's natural sparkle became his trademark. Some of it would eventually rub off on his teammates.

He certainly brought a smile to their faces during the warm-up period of his first-ever NBA game.

"As the hot new rookie, I was given the honor of leading the Lakers onto the court for the pregame warm-ups," he said. All he had to do was dribble the ball down the court and dunk it in the basket. "That wasn't hard, but I was still nervous. After all, this was the first game of my professional career."

His entrance didn't go quite as smoothly as he'd hoped:

"When it was time for the Lakers to come out on the floor, I took the ball, drove to the basket, and—boom—fell flat on my face. I had tripped over my warm-up pants.... My teammates found this absolutely hysterical."

MAGIC MOMENT

When Magic Johnson joined the Los Angeles Lakers, Kareem Abdul-Jabbar was top dog—and Kareem wore jersey number 33, Magic's college number. Kareem wasn't about to change his shirt, so Magic became number 32, the same number he had worn in high school.

KING KAREEM

Kareem Abdul-Jabbar was born Ferdinand Lewis Alcindor Jr. in New York City in 1947. Always the tallest kid in his class, Lew excelled in basketball throughout high school and college. In 1969, everyone knew that he would be the first choice in the NBA draft. He was picked by the Milwaukee Bucks, who were in their second year as an NBA franchise. The Bucks had won a highly publicized coin-toss with the Phoenix Suns, who were also in their second year, and with it, the right to choose Lew.

In their second season, and the first with Lew aboard, the Bucks went from a seventh-place finish in their division (without Lew) to the second-best record in the entire league. That same year, Lew was named NBA Rookie of the Year. In 1970–1971, with Lew in his second season, the Bucks hit the jackpot. After winning their division and conference titles, they moved on to the NBA Finals, where they defeated the Baltimore Bullets in four straight games.

Lew, who had been raised a Roman Catholic but converted to Islam while in college, changed his name to Kareem Abdul-Jabbar the day after the Bucks won the 1971 NBA championship. He helped the Bucks make the playoffs for the next three years. In 1974, Kareem and the Bucks again played for the NBA championship, losing to the Boston Celtics in the seventh game.

In 1975, Kareem was traded to the Los Angeles Lakers, with whom he played for 14 years. As a Laker, Kareem added five more NBA championships to the one

Magic stood up with a smile, believing "things could only improve from here."

Instead, he played so badly in the early part of the game that Coach Jack McKinney pulled him off the court after just nine minutes. Fortunately, Jack gave him another chance late in the game. By then, Magic had settled down, and he played well.

When Kareem made a basket to win the game just as the buzzer sounded, Magic was so excited, he ran to the "big guy," jumped into his arms and hugged him. Kareem, one of the most emotionally controlled NBA players, was not amused. He told Magic to calm down. "But I wasn't about to change my style," said Magic.

he had won with Milwaukee, added three league MVPs for a league-record total of six, and added a Championship Finals MVP to the one he had already won with the Bucks.

When he retired in 1989 at age 42, Kareem held many NBA records—most points scored, most field goals, and most NBA games played, among others. His jersey (number 33) has been retired by both the Bucks and the Lakers.

Since leaving the NBA, Kareem has done some coaching, written several books, worked to fight hunger and illiteracy, and promoted causes related to social justice and African-American history. He has been honored for numerous causes, including promoting equality and African-American history, and for raising awareness for cancer research. He's even done some acting, sometimes playing himself and taking comic roles. These are all the more entertaining when contrasted with the serious side that he presented throughout his NBA career.

In 2016, ESPN ranked him second (after Michael Jordan) in its All-Time NBA Top 100 list.

Over the course of Kareem Abdul-Jabbar's long, illustrious career, protective goggles and his skyhook shot became two of his claims to fame. Top: In the 1974–1975 season, while playing for the Milwaukee Bucks, Kareem suffered a scratched eye and began wearing goggles for protection. Bottom: By the late 1980s, around the time this photo was taken and the end of his career playing alongside Magic Johnson as a Los Angeles Laker, Kareem's goggles had become considerably more sleek than the ones he first wore with the Bucks.

"I'd always played with passion, and eventually my teammates would get used to it."

Over the years, even stoic Kareem would give Magic the occasional high-five!

After that awkward first outing with the Lakers, Magic proved the team was right to have believed in him.

In his first year in the NBA, Magic and the Lakers played so well throughout the season and into the post-season playoffs that they finished first in both their division and the Western Conference. Their victory in the Western Conference Finals put the team into the NBA Finals for the first time in seven years. The 1980 best-of-seven series pitted the Lakers against the Philadelphia 76ers.

During Game 5, team leader Kareem sprained his ankle, taking him out for the rest of the series. At that point, the Lakers were ahead three games to two. Without Kareem, though, basketball insiders believed the Lakers had no hope of winning.

At the start of Game 6, Coach Paul Westhead—who had taken the place of Jack McKinney when Jack suffered a near-fatal head injury earlier in the season—surprised everyone, including Magic. He announced that the rookie would start in Kareem's position, as center. Even though he hadn't played center since high school, Magic rose to the challenge. In the end, he played all five positions during the game, leading his team to victory—and the NBA championship.

"I had the game of my life," said Magic. "I played 47 minutes out of 48, and finished with 42 points, 15 rebounds, and seven assists. I shot 14 free throws and hit every one."

By the end of his rookie season, Magic had helped the Lakers overcome huge odds in the Finals, led the team to the NBA championship, and earned himself championship-series MVP honors. Here, the 1980 NBA champion Los Angeles Lakers pose for a team photo. Front row, left to right: Chairman of the Board Jerry Buss, Spencer Haywood, Jamaal Wilkes, Kareem Abdul-Jabbar, Magic Johnson, Jim Chones, and General Manager Bill Sharman. Back row: Head Coach Paul Westhead, Butch Lee, Brad Holland, Mark Landsberger, Marty Byrnes, Michael Cooper, Norm Nixon, Trainer Jack Curran, and Assistant Coach Pat Riley.

The icing on the cake came when he was named MVP of the championship series—the first rookie ever to earn that honor. The game is still considered one of the best of his entire career. Said Coach Westhead after the game:

"Magic is truly Houdini. He is a magic man. Everybody thinks of Magic as a fancy type of player—the kind of guy who makes the behind-the-back pass or the dazzling play. But in reality, he's our blue-collar worker. He goes out there and works hard and ... never gives up until the game is over. He's one of a kind."

BIGGER, FASTER, STRONGER

Just as Magic had to adjust his basketball playing style when he moved from high school to college, he had to adapt again when he joined the NBA. "The level of play is a lot higher in the pros," he said. "The NBA is a business, with big money, big stakes, and big egos."

The players may enjoy playing the game, but basketball is also their livelihood—they need to be high performers to keep their jobs. Players are bigger, stronger, and more competitive. Injuries are more common—and often more serious—in the NBA than in the NCAA.

In college ball, teams play 30 regular-season games. In the NBA, they play 82 games. In addition are preseason exhibition games and postseason playoff games. All those games add up to a lot of late nights in front of fans, followed by early-morning practices and exhausting travel schedules. Magic learned to nap in the afternoons.

An NBA game is also eight minutes longer, with four 12-minute quarters, compared to the NCAA's two 20-minute halves. There are a few different rules, making it a faster-paced, higher-scoring game.

One of the biggest changes, said Magic, is that "you come out of college as a big star, and suddenly you're at the bottom again. You have to learn to be humble."

The Magic Fades

Magic's second season in the NBA was the complete opposite of his debut year. In November 1980, he injured his knee, forcing him to sit out 45 games—more than half the season. It was the first time in his career he had been seriously injured. He had knee surgery, followed by months of painful recovery. During that time, he was alone and idle. He missed his teammates and playing ball. "It's the most down I've ever been," he said.

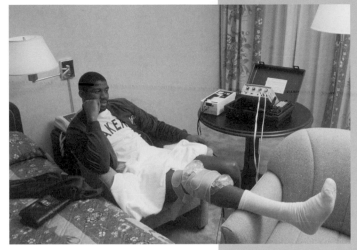

A dejected-looking Magic Johnson sits in a hotel room with his injured knee wrapped in bandages and ice packs, and hooked up to monitoring equipment.

Magic returned in time for the Western Conference playoffs, but the Houston Rockets knocked the Lakers out of the series in the first round. At the same time, a conflict between Magic and one of his teammates was played out—very publicly and unprofessionally—in the media.

"My second season with the Lakers was the worst year I've ever had in basketball," said Magic. "And the first couple of months of the following season were even worse."

In the summer of 1981, even though Magic had only played 37 games the previous season, team owner Jerry Buss offered him a 25-year, $25-million contract. At the time, it was the longest, richest contract in American sports history. Jerry's goal was to ensure that Magic had a solid income long after his playing days were over.

Within a few months, though, Magic had become fed up with Coach Paul Westhead and his approach to the game, which Magic claimed had made the Lakers "slow" and "predictable." The team had started the season with a poor record, and Magic believed Paul's methods would lead to more losses.

One night, in November 1981, after the Lakers fought for a slim win over the Utah Jazz, the 22-year-old player blew up in the locker room—in front of reporters. "I can't play here any more," he said. "I want to leave. I want to be traded." Then he stormed out of the room, still wearing his uniform. He said he was going to see Jerry.

The following day, Jerry fired Coach Westhead, replacing him with assistant coach Pat Riley. Jerry insisted that Magic's ill-timed outburst had nothing to do with the change in coaching staff. "The irony, which makes what Magic did unfortunate, is that I had already decided to fire [Paul]. But I don't think anyone will ever totally believe that."

The fans sure didn't believe it. As far as they were concerned, Magic Johnson, the 25-million-dollar-man, was a high-paid, selfish brat who had just gotten a good coach fired. They booed him at games. The *L.A. Times* printed letters-to-the-editor from basketball fans, who called him a "crybaby," "a prima donna," and a "glory-hog." One letter read: "I can't believe it. A winning coach is fired because an overpaid, spoiled-rotten superstar has a temper tantrum."

Magic wasn't used to being the bad guy, and he hated being cast in the role. He hated the booing. He hated that fans thought he was dishonorable.

Eventually, of course, he won them back—largely because under new coach Pat Riley, the L.A. Lakers returned to their winning ways. In spring 1982, the team won another NBA championship—again beating the 76ers. Magic also repeated his post-season MVP win.

Showtime

With Jerry Buss at the helm, Pat Riley coaching, and superstars Magic Johnson and Kareem Abdul-Jabbar on the courts, the Lakers began to dominate the NBA. An era dubbed "Showtime" was born.

During this dazzling period in Lakers history—from the fall of 1981, when Pat became coach, to the spring of 1989, when Kareem retired—the Lakers won four NBA championships. They

Pat Riley was the Lakers' head coach during most of the team's 1980s "Showtime" era. His tailored suits and slicked-back hair fit in well with the Lakers' image as a "Hollywood" team, and his love for the running game suited the team's fast-paced style on the court.

played in the NBA Finals every season except 1985–1986.

With Magic's remarkable passing ability and Kareem's equally remarkable shooting ability, the Lakers played fast, high-scoring games. The players were so connected on-court that they seemed to sense, rather than see, each other. They made apparently impossible plays that baffled their opponents.

The team was energetic, exciting, and innovative. But Showtime wasn't just about the on-court action.

To liven up home games at the L.A. Forum, team owner Jerry Buss brought in an energetic announcer, a ten-piece band, and a squad of cheerleaders. He lured Hollywood stars into the stands and transformed the Forum Club, formerly a family restaurant, into the hottest nightclub in town.

On game nights, everyone who was anyone was at the Forum. The arena was no longer merely home to a basketball court. During the Showtime era, the Forum was a glitzy, star-studded entertainment hub that altered the image of the NBA.

Meanwhile, on the other side of the country, another NBA superpower treated its fans to its own version of an electrifying show. The Boston Celtics, with superstar Larry Bird, were to the East Coast what the Lakers and Magic Johnson were to the West Coast.

Because the league was split up into conferences based mostly on geography, the Celtics and the Lakers only met on-court twice during the regular season. Despite that, sports reporters continually compared the two star

In 1979, Lakers owner Jerry Buss decided to turn the L.A. Forum into a place where fans could look forward not only to a fast game on the court, but also to fun and excitement during time outs and in the seating areas. He hired performers to entertain customers in the aisles, and on the court he assembled a group of talented dancers who cheered the team and performed during time outs. Called the Laker Girls (shown here), they were part of the larger entertainment package of the Showtime era and inspired other teams to produce the kinds of routines that are common throughout the NBA today. Laker games also became, and remain today, see-and-be-seen events where celebrities can be spotted in the seats. Probably the longest-standing celebrity fan, and most recognizable sitting courtside in his trademark sunglasses, is actor Jack Nicholson (inset).

players. Who scored more points? Who did fans prefer—flashy Magic, or hard-working Larry? Which of them was the better player? The media portrayed Magic and Larry as arch rivals, building a hostility between them that didn't necessarily exist in person.

> *"During my career in the NBA, I've gone up against hundreds, maybe even thousands of players. Many were good. A few were very good. A tiny handful even deserved to be called great. But there was nobody greater than Larry Bird."*
>
> Earvin "Magic" Johnson, *My Life*, 1992

Finally, in spring 1984, came the battle fans had been awaiting for five years—Larry Bird and Magic Johnson were to meet face to face in a final, for the first time since college.

"This was the matchup that everybody wanted," including the teams, said Magic. "It had been fifteen years since the Lakers and Celtics had met in the Finals. There had been a total of seven championship series between our two teams. And in all that time, the Lakers had never won."

As it turned out, this was not to be the year the Lakers ended the curse of the Celtics. They lost the series, four games to three.

A year later, the two teams faced off again. This time, the Lakers came out on top, winning Game 6—and the series—in Boston. "The

[Boston] fans were stunned," said Magic. "They didn't really believe that such a thing was possible. Never before in Celtic history had Boston lost a championship series on their home court."

In the 1985–1986 season, the Lakers began the season strong with a 24–3 start and won their fifth straight division title. However, they were beaten in the Western Conference Finals, by the Houston Rockets, whom Boston went on to defeat for the NBA championship.

In 1987, the Lakers and the Celtics met in the NBA Finals for what would be the last time in the Magic Johnson-Larry Bird era. Again, the Lakers won, four games to two.

Larry Bird and Magic Johnson fight for rebound position in game two of the 1985 NBA Finals between the Celtics and the Lakers. This time, it would be Los Angeles beating Boston, four games to two.

Larry Bird and Magic Johnson clown around at a photo shoot during the 1984 NBA Finals in Los Angeles. Larry's polishing of the trophy turned out to be prophetic, as his Boston Celtics defeated Magic's Los Angeles Lakers, winning the series, and the trophy, four games to three.

In 1987, as an added bonus for Magic, he was named Finals MVP for the third time, and regular-season MVP for the first time in his career. It was "the one prize that had always eluded me," he said. "After eight years in the pros, I finally won the [season] MVP award. Larry had already won it three times, but who's counting?"

Magic is doused with champagne during the Lakers' victory celebration following their 1987 championship win over Boston. Magic had already been named league MVP for the season and had just received the Finals MVP.

Before he retired from the NBA, Magic would win the league MVP award twice more (1989 and 1990), tying Larry's final tally. He also won one more NBA championship with the Lakers—in 1988, against the Detroit Pistons in a seven-game series. With that win, the Lakers became the first team to win back-to-back titles since the Celtics had done so in 1968 and 1969.

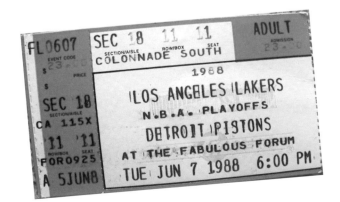

THE RIVALRY CONTINUES

The rivalry between basketball wizards Magic Johnson and Larry Bird began in college in the late 1970s. It continued through the 1980s, as they faced each other on opposite sides of NBA courts. Two decades later, the competition between the two players moved to a new venue—a Broadway theater stage.

In 2012, a play called *Magic/Bird* opened at the Longacre Theater in New York City. Written by author and director Eric Simonson, the play was about the longtime rivalry—and friendship—between the two celebrated athletes. Unfortunately, it didn't last as long as their relationship has. The play closed after running for only six weeks.

Magic Moment

After the L.A. Lakers won the 1987 NBA Finals, it would be 21 years before the Boston Celtics had a chance to even the score. The next time the two teams met in an NBA final, in 2008, Boston won. Since then, the two teams have played against each other in just one more NBA championship series. The Lakers took that trophy in 2010.

After the 1988 championship series win against Detroit, the Lakers' fortunes began a slow but, as it would turn out, steady decline.

The team made the playoffs in each of the next three seasons. In 1989, they made the NBA Finals, but hampered by injuries to Magic and teammate Byron Scott, they were swept by Detroit in four straight games.

On June 28, 1989, following the Lakers' loss to Detroit, Kareem Abdul-Jabbar retired from the NBA at age 42.

In 1990, the Lakers lost to the Phoenix Suns in the second round of the playoffs, four games to one. Following his team's failure to make it past the second round, head coach Pat Riley stepped down.

In 1991, under new head coach Mike Dunleavy, the Lakers again made it to the NBA Finals. This time they lost to Michael Jordan and the Chicago Bulls, four games to one.

With the departure of such key figures as Kareem Abdul-Jabbar and Pat Riley, Showtime was all but over for the Lakers. A shocking announcement from Magic Johnson in the fall of 1991 shut down the magical era once and for all.

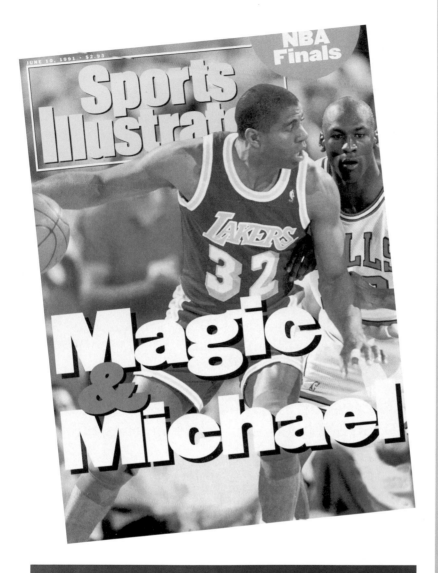

This Sports Illustrated *cover shows Magic Johnson driving against the Chicago Bulls' Michael Jordan during the 1991 NBA Finals.*

"No one was more dynamic, or magical, with the ball in the open court than Earvin Johnson. He lifted the Lakers, and transition basketball, to ethereal levels. He was transcendent."

ESPN reporter Rob Peterson, 2016

Chapter 5
Changing Course

O n November 7, 1991, Magic Johnson held one of the most memorable press conferences in American sports history. That day, he announced to the world that he was HIV-positive, and was retiring from the NBA. At the time, the common belief was that HIV automatically led to AIDS—and AIDS was a death sentence. Magic made it clear, though, that he did not have AIDS, and he had no intention of allowing the illness to get the better of him. "I plan on going on living for a long time," he said. "It's another challenge, another chapter in my life... I'm going to go on, I'm going to beat it, and I'm going to have fun."

Magic announces to the world that he has tested positive for HIV, the virus that can cause AIDS. His wife Cookie sits next to the podium, on the left side of the photo.

Magic's New Reality

At Magic's side the day he made his life-changing announcement was his wife Earleatha, better known to everyone as "Cookie." She and Magic had only been married for two months, but they had known each other for 14 years. They had met as first-year students at Michigan State just before Christmas 1977. They had gone on their first date in January 1978. Said Magic of those early days in their relationship:

"After the first week with Cookie, I just knew I would marry her. I never told her that, of course. I hid my feelings. But I knew in my heart that we would be together for a long time."

Despite that belief, as an 18-year-old college kid, Magic made it clear to Cookie that he was not a one-woman man. He told her he planned to continue dating other women—and for the next 14 years, he did just that. During those years, he and Cookie broke up and reunited

over and over again. Twice, they were even engaged to be married—and twice Magic called off the weddings.

At last, in September 1991, Magic said he finally "wised up and married Cookie."

During the couple's on-and-off years, Magic had sexual relations

Around the time that Magic announced he was HIV-positive, he and his wife Cookie discovered that she was pregnant. Cookie was frightened for her own safety and that of her unborn son, but it turned out that both she and her baby were healthy. Throughout the days, months, and years to come, she has stood by Magic and partnered with him in his work to raise understanding and money in the fight against HIV/AIDS.

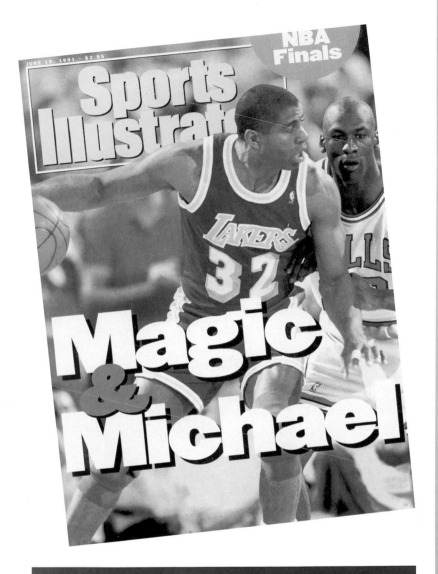

This Sports Illustrated cover shows Magic Johnson driving against the Chicago Bulls' Michael Jordan during the 1991 NBA Finals.

"No one was more dynamic, or magical, with the ball in the open court than Earvin Johnson. He lifted the Lakers, and transition basketball, to ethereal levels. He was transcendent."

ESPN reporter Rob Peterson, 2016

Chapter 5
Changing Course

On November 7, 1991, Magic Johnson held one of the most memorable press conferences in American sports history. That day, he announced to the world that he was HIV-positive, and was retiring from the NBA. At the time, the common belief was that HIV automatically led to AIDS—and AIDS was a death sentence. Magic made it clear, though, that he did not have AIDS, and he had no intention of allowing the illness to get the better of him. "I plan on going on living for a long time," he said. "It's another challenge, another chapter in my life... I'm going to go on, I'm going to beat it, and I'm going to have fun."

Magic announces to the world that he has tested positive for HIV, the virus that can cause AIDS. His wife Cookie sits next to the podium, on the left side of the photo.

Magic's New Reality

At Magic's side the day he made his life-changing announcement was his wife Earleatha, better known to everyone as "Cookie." She and Magic had only been married for two months, but they had known each other for 14 years. They had met as first-year students at Michigan State just before Christmas 1977. They had gone on their first

date in January 1978. Said Magic of those early days in their relationship:

"After the first week with Cookie, I just knew I would marry her. I never told her that, of course. I hid my feelings. But I knew in my heart that we would be together for a long time."

Despite that belief, as an 18-year-old college kid, Magic made it clear to Cookie that he was not a one-woman man. He told her he planned to continue dating other women—and for the next 14 years, he did just that. During those years, he and Cookie broke up and reunited

over and over again. Twice, they were even engaged to be married—and twice Magic called off the weddings.

At last, in September 1991, Magic said he finally "wised up and married Cookie."

During the couple's on-and-off years, Magic had sexual relations

Around the time that Magic announced he was HIV-positive, he and his wife Cookie discovered that she was pregnant. Cookie was frightened for her own safety and that of her unborn son, but it turned out that both she and her baby were healthy. Throughout the days, months, and years to come, she has stood by Magic and partnered with him in his work to raise understanding and money in the fight against HIV/AIDS.

with many, many women. He even fathered a child with one of them. Cookie knew all of this when she married Magic. What she didn't know at the time—nor did he—was that he had contracted HIV from one of his sexual partners.

As soon as Magic walked through the door of their Los Angeles home that night, Cookie knew something was terribly wrong. When her husband told her about the diagnosis, "I was scared," she said. "I cried a lot... I couldn't believe it."

Magic told his wife he would understand if she wanted to end their marriage. Her reaction? "I smacked him lightly on the face. 'Are you crazy?' I said. 'Why do you think I married you? I married you because I love you!'" She told him they would fight this battle together.

Two days later, Cookie was tested for HIV. "The good news—no the great news—was that Cookie was fine," wrote Magic in his 1992 autobiography, *My Life*. That meant that the couple's unborn baby, too, was in the clear.

"*People make all kinds of choices in their lives. Some drink. Some smoke. Some eat too much. That wasn't me. My pleasure was being with women. All of this happened during my long, on-again, off-again relationship with Cookie.... I was a single guy in my twenties. I had a job that took a lot out of me, both at home and on the road. And aside from hanging out with my teammates, one of my favorite ways to relax was being with women. And I guess the feeling was mutual. The longer I played in the NBA, the more women seemed to be attracted to me.*"

Earvin "Magic" Johnson, *My Life*, 1992

What the HIV diagnosis meant for Magic, though, was that he had to take time off from the game he loved. He needed time to focus on his health. Doctors advised him that HIV was not necessarily fatal. If Magic took the prescribed medication, looked after himself, and maintained a positive attitude, he might be able to live a long life. He was to continue exercising—but not at the pace required for a career in professional basketball.

> *"When [the doctor] first announced it to me, I thought: 'Oh, man, I am going to die. I think it's over.'"*
>
> Magic Johnson, upon hearing his HIV diagnosis

For the first two weeks following his diagnosis, Magic pretended he had the flu to explain his absences from Lakers' practices and games. "It was the first time I'd ever missed the opening game of the season," he said. He spent the time gathering information about his illness, meeting with doctors, and planning a public announcement. He also quietly shared the news with family, close friends, coaches, and Lakers' management.

Despite everyone's best efforts to keep Magic's illness quiet, sports reporters who knew him realized something was up. They knew a flu wouldn't last two weeks. They began calling and asking questions. Magic knew he couldn't wait any longer to announce his diagnosis to the world.

On November 7, just before the press conference began, Magic gathered his Lakers teammates in the locker room to give them the bad news. He wanted them to hear it from him,

Teammates, fans, and other members of the public were hit hard by Magic's announcement that he had tested positive for HIV and would be retiring from basketball. In this photo, members of the boys' basketball team at Fairfax High School fight back tears as they listen to a radio broadcast of Magic's press conference on November 7, 1991.

not from reporters. "Until then, I hadn't cried," he said. "But when I told my teammates what was going on, they were in tears." One by one, the players hugged their longtime point guard. "I cried with them," said Magic.

Ninety minutes later, he walked into the room where the press conference was to be held. "There were more reporters and cameramen than I had ever seen before," he said. "Meanwhile, hundreds of fans had gathered outside the building... The news was already out."

A New Mission in Life

At the press conference, Magic admitted he would miss playing basketball, but he now had a more important mission in life—to advocate

MAGIC MOMENT

In 2004, as part of its 25th anniversary celebrations, sports network ESPN created a list of The 100 Most Memorable Moments of the Past 25 Years. Magic Johnson's HIV announcement ranked number seven on that list.

THE LEADING MAN

In 1985, Hollywood heartthrob Rock Hudson (shown here in the 1976 science fiction/horror movie *Embryo*) died two months after announcing to the world that he had AIDS. The handsome actor was the first major celebrity to succumb to AIDS-related illness.

By the time he died, Rock had appeared in about 70 movies and starred in a number of popular TV shows. When he announced his illness, his celebrity caused the public to pay attention.

Like Magic Johnson's announcement, Rock Hudson's revelation raised awareness of HIV and AIDS. Donations flooded into AIDS-related organizations. A few weeks before Rock's death, though, it was made public that he had been involved in homosexual relationships. That helped further the belief that AIDS was exclusively a gay man's disease. At the time, this was a belief many people held throughout North America—at least until Magic made his announcement five years later.

for people living with HIV and AIDS, and to educate young people about the importance of safe sex.

He also wanted people to know that HIV and AIDS could touch anyone—including a wealthy, married, African-American basketball hero.

"In 1991, many Americans remained convinced that AIDS was a disease that affected gay, white men—people like [actor] Rock Hudson—but almost nobody else," wrote Michael Specter in *The New Yorker* in 2014. "There was no better way to demonstrate that HIV is a virus that can attack anyone than for one of America's most electrifying athletes to acknowledge that he was infected."

As awful as the basketball star's diagnosis was, physicians and others working in the medical community knew a person of his celebrity could make a huge difference in the fight against HIV and AIDS. A day or so after Magic's announcement, prominent AIDS researcher Anthony S. Fauci said:

"This had happened to me, and there wasn't too much I could do about that. But there was a great deal I could do for other people. By going public with this, I had a chance to save lives."

Earvin "Magic" Johnson, *My Life*, 1992

"If Magic helps, we can use this terrible tragedy to make some young people listen to the truth in a way they may never have before.... [T]his will be an opportunity to remind people that HIV is not a hopeless disease. There are treatments, and the sooner people seek them, the more likely they are to benefit. If [Magic] can help bring this lesson home, he will influence more lives than he ever did with basketball."

True to his word, Magic immediately began working to change public attitudes toward HIV and AIDS. The day after his press conference, he appeared on a national talk show hosted by his friend Arsenio Hall, and had an in-depth interview with *Sports Illustrated* magazine. He called for young people to practice safe sex and to get tested for HIV.

A Good Friend at a Tough Time

Magic Johnson first met Arsenio Hall soon after he moved to Los Angeles. At the time, Arsenio was paying his dues as a stand-up comedian, and Magic was finding his way in his new hometown. Over the years, as their respective success and fame increased, the two became close friends.

From 1989 to 1994, Arsenio hosted a popular late-night TV talk show, *The Arsenio Hall Show*. After Magic made his HIV announcement, he turned to Arsenio to help get his message out. He wanted his first post-press conference interview to be "with somebody I knew and trusted."

Within days of announcing that he had tested HIV-positive, Magic began working to change public attitudes about HIV/AIDS. Here, he is shown in a TV appearance with his friend and talk-show host Arsenio Hall.

He got so many letters of support—and so many unsolicited donations—that within two weeks of his press conference, he launched the Magic Johnson Foundation to fund HIV/AIDS education and research.

In mid-November, then-U.S. President George Bush asked Magic to join the National Commission on AIDS. Magic accepted the position, but resigned in frustration ten months later because the commission's "important work [was] utterly ignored by [the Bush] administration."

In spring 1992, Magic wrote a book called *What You Can Do to Avoid AIDS*, he and Arsenio produced an AIDS awareness video called *Time Out*, and he appeared on an AIDS special for children called *A Conversation with Magic*.

Magic's goal with all these projects was to educate people about HIV/AIDS, especially young African Americans. "I'm trying to make sure that what happened to me doesn't happen to them," he said.

Magic's revelation about his HIV status had another, unexpected, side effect. "Within a month of Magic Johnson's announcement, the number of people seeking HIV tests in New York City rose by sixty per cent," wrote Michael Specter in *The New Yorker*. "A similarly sharp increase was noted in many cities throughout the nation."

Because of Magic Johnson, Americans were openly discussing HIV, educating themselves, and getting tested.

THE MAGIC JOHNSON FOUNDATION

In 1991, shortly after he learned he was HIV-positive, Magic Johnson created the Magic Johnson Foundation (MJF) to raise money for HIV/AIDS education and research. Over the years, the organization has branched out. Now, its goal is to address the "educational, health and social needs of ethnically diverse, urban communities," reads the MJF website.

The group still works to raise awareness of, and help prevent, HIV/AIDS. In addition, it now provides scholarships, mentorships, and internships to exceptional "minority students," and supports 16 Community Empowerment Centers across the country. These venues provide education, technology, and employment support to low-income individuals of all ages.

So far, the Magic Johnson Foundation has raised and donated more than $20 million to various causes. It touches more than 250,000 people a year.

> *"The 1991–92 season turned out to be the most productive one I ever had. Only instead of playing basketball, I was now playing a new position in a very different game. Instead of being a point guard, I was an activist, and especially an educator. And instead of being a veteran, I was starting all over again as a rookie."*
>
> Earvin "Magic" Johnson,
> *My Life*, 1992

Meanwhile, Back on the B-Ball Court ...

Even though Magic had switched his focus to HIV/AIDS awareness and activism, he just couldn't stay away from basketball—and his fans didn't want him to.

Three months after his "retirement" from the NBA, Magic was back on the court—playing in the annual NBA All-Star Game. Every year, fans and coaches choose 12 of the best players from both the Eastern and the Western conferences to face off in one star-studded game. The game usually takes place in mid-February.

In early 1992, Magic was no longer playing for the Lakers, but fans voted him onto the Western Conference All-Star team anyway. It was his 12th career All-Star appearance, but this time, the game held more meaning than usual:

"I was thrilled... I deserved one last game. As much as I wanted to play for the fans, I was also there for myself. I wanted to prove that I could still play this game, that I could play it as well as I had before this virus came along."

The game was important to the NBA, too, wrote sportswriter Roland Lazenby: "Suddenly, it wasn't just another boring All-Star Game. It was Magic Johnson's grand finale, the farewell event, the greatest public relations opportunity that AIDS awareness campaigners could imagine."

In the lead-up to the game, the NBA launched "a massive information campaign, for both athletes and the media," wrote Lazenby. The game itself was called "emotional," "riveting," and "inspirational" by other sportswriters.

Magic Johnson flashes his famous smile during the February 1992 NBA All-Star Game in Orlando, Florida. Despite not having played for the Lakers since his announced retirement the previous fall, fans voted him onto the West squad. Magic responded with a performance for the ages. He led all scorers with 25 points and won the game MVP trophy. In a moving tribute to Magic, as he scored the last of three straight three-point shots with 14.5 seconds left in the game, players from both squads let the game end on that stirring, memorable note.

Magic was nervous going into the contest. "I hadn't played a real game in ages," he said. Plus, he knew the game was being broadcast to thousands of people around the globe. "I wanted to show the world that people with HIV could still run, jump, and play basketball."

He did just that, leading his Western Conference All-Star team to a 153–113 win over the East, and earning the game MVP trophy.

Magic Johnson's jersey (number 32) hangs in the Staples Center with those of other Lakers whose numbers have been retired.

Magic mugs for the camera during a photo shoot with fellow Olympians (and Dream Team members) Larry Bird (number 7) and Michael Jordan (number 9) at the 1992 Summer Olympics in Barcelona, Spain.

A week after the All-Star game, the Los Angeles Lakers retired Magic's number 32 in an emotional ceremony. Little did the team know, the number would be coming out of retirement soon enough.

In August 1992, Magic was on-court again, this time playing for Olympic gold with the U.S. men's basketball team in Barcelona, Spain. In addition to Magic, the U.S. team roster included such legendary players as Michael Jordan, Charles Barkley, and Magic's longtime rival, Larry Bird. It was the first time professional basketball players had been allowed to play in the Olympic Games. With its high-powered squad, the U.S. team, nicknamed the "Dream Team," easily won gold.

Karl Malone of the Utah Jazz was one of the most outspoken players expressing doubts about Magic's intention to return to basketball in 1992.

Despite having won high school, NCAA, and NBA titles, Magic said that having the Olympic medal placed around his neck was "the greatest feeling I've ever felt winning anything."

By this time, Magic was considering a comeback to the NBA. His doctors approved, as long as he didn't play the full 82-game schedule. On September 29, 1992, Magic Johnson held yet another press conference. "I'm back," he announced. Number 32 was coming out of retirement.

Over the next few weeks, Magic played five preseason games with the Lakers—but a controversy about his HIV status had begun to brew. Throughout the NBA, people were split over whether Magic should be allowed to play. Some players and coaches reportedly expressed concerns, anonymously, about the health risks involved with Magic on the court. One of Magic's teammates told *The New York Times* that some players in the league "wished Magic would just go away."

This "sniping from players," as the *Times* called it, increased after Magic cut his arm—and bled—during a game against the Cleveland Cavaliers on Friday, October 30.

After that, Karl Malone of the Utah Jazz said publically "that he had very real concerns about his health and the health of other players being compromised if Magic continued to play," reported the *Times*.

Most doctors and researchers feel that the chances of getting HIV through casual contact between two athletes (other than boxers) who had cut themselves are so small as to be almost nonexistent. There is always some danger of many kinds of infection being transmitted through blood. But in most cases involving HIV, there would have to be a significant amount of blood. Also, the blood would have to do more than lie on the skin, where exposure to the air would cause the blood to dry and the virus to die. Any blood on the outside of the body would have to become absorbed fairly quickly into the bloodstream. This is very unlikely without something actually forcing the blood beneath the skin. This is why the risk of infection by liquids containing HIV-contaminated blood in needles is so high.

Magic Johnson gives Doug Christie a pat on the back during Magic's first game as head coach of the Lakers in March 1994.

The growing debate wasn't good for the NBA—nor was it healthy for Magic. "I could see what lay ahead," he said. "Every time I came into another city, the controversy and the fear would start all over again." Basketball would no longer be the focus of a game because "Everybody would be too busy putting in their two cents about whether I should be playing."

The controversy also posed a potential threat to Magic's health. "If I'm going to beat this virus, I've got to avoid pressure and stress. That's the last thing I need in my life."

With that in mind, on November 3, 1992—at his second press conference in six weeks—Magic Johnson announced he was retiring again. Still, he promised reporters and his fans, "I'll never disappear. I don't know how to."

On-Again, Off-Again with the Lakers

After announcing his second retirement, Magic spent his time promoting his just-released bestselling autobiography, *My Life*, working as an NBA commentator, and running Magic Johnson Enterprises—a business he had launched in 1987.

In March 1994, Lakers' owner Jerry Buss convinced Magic to step in as interim coach for the team. Things started off well enough, with Magic coaching the players to five wins in their next six games. After that, though, it was loss after loss for the Lakers. They ended the season on a 10-game losing streak, leaving Magic's coaching record at 5–11. Magic immediately gave up coaching. It was a position he had not actually sought, and had only taken at Jerry's urging.

Over the years, Jerry had shared with Magic the inside workings of the Lakers' organization and introduced him to prominent Los Angeles businesspeople. In June 1994, after Magic had decided to quit coaching, Jerry sold him a 5 percent share in the Lakers, making Magic a part owner and team executive.

It turned out, though, that the legendary point guard wasn't finished on the court just yet. Not even two years later, he sold his shares so he could play ball again. (Players are not allowed to be team owners.)

Magic, then 36 years old, played the final three months of the regular 1995–1996 season, and in the first round of the 1996 NBA playoffs. By then, though, the six-foot-nine-inch (206-cm) former superstar had lost the magic.

"Stronger and bigger, Johnson was still a gifted passer, but he was also a step slower, especially on defense," reported *the New York Times* in May 1996. In addition, said the *Times*,

MAGIC MOMENT

In 1994, between retirements from the NBA, Magic founded the Magic Johnson All-Stars. This team of former NBA and NCAA stars played exhibition games against teams from all over the world. Playing with this team in 2001, Magic appeared in his first game in the Lansing, Michigan, area since he'd left Michigan State 22 years earlier. Performing in a sold-out arena, 42-year-old Magic played the entire game and had a triple-double. This time, he played against his former team, the Michigan State Spartans. The Spartans won the game by two points. A year later, Magic filled his All-Stars roster with members of a touring Australian team and returned to East Lansing, beating the Spartans, 104–85.

Magic clashed with fellow players, earned a two-game suspension "for bumping a referee," and criticized coaches.

After the Lakers lost the opening playoff series to the Houston Rockets, Magic once again called it quits—for real this time.

"It's time to move on," he said. "I'm going out on my terms, something I couldn't say when I aborted a comeback in 1992."

Within a few months, Magic bought back his shares in the team. He maintained his part-ownership status until 2010. That year, in "a bittersweet business decision," he sold his interest in the Lakers—but he still didn't cut his ties with the team. He stayed on as an unpaid vice president for another four years.

For almost ten years after his 1996 retirement, even though he no longer played in the NBA, Magic continued to play basketball. He traveled around the world with the Magic Johnson All-Stars, a barnstorming, or touring, team he had formed in 1994. He also briefly joined a Swedish basketball team, then a Danish team.

During this decade, he also wrote two more books, earned a place in the Naismith Memorial Basketball Hall of Fame, and hosted a short-lived late-night talk show.

Mostly, Magic poured his time and energy into his business interests and continued to raise awareness—and money—to combat HIV/AIDS.

MAGIC MOMENT

In 1998, Magic launched his own talk show. It turns out this was one thing he wasn't so "magic" at. *The Magic Hour* was canceled after two months because of low ratings.

The Magic Johnson All-Stars stopped their barnstorming tours sometime around 2002. In 2003, Magic found one more way to make his presence felt on the court when he signed a one-dollar-for-life contract with the world-renowned "Clown Princes of Basketball"—the Harlem Globetrotters. Here he is shown clowning around with the crowd during an exhibition game between the Globetrotters and the Spartans of Michigan State. The game, which the Globetrotters won, extended their current winning streak to 283 games. It was also payback for a Spartans' victory in 2000 that snapped what was at the time a 1,270-game Globetrotters' winning streak. During the game pictured here, the day was marked by a moving halftime tribute to Magic and other members of the Spartans' 1979 NCAA championship team.

ALL IN THE FAMILY

Magic's first child, André, was born in 1981. André grew up in Lansing, Michigan, with his mother Melissa Mitchell. Although he was raised by his mom, André Johnson spent a great deal of time with his father. Today, he is an executive at Magic Johnson Enterprises.

In September 1991, Magic married his longtime love Earleatha "Cookie" Kelly. Together, the couple has two children—Earvin III, known as "EJ," and Elisa.

EJ was born in June 1992. Today, he is well known as a character on the reality TV show *Rich Kids of Beverly Hills*. He has also made a name for himself as a fashion icon, appearing as a correspondent on a show called *Fashion Police*. In 2013, he announced to the world that he is gay. Two years later, he made news again when he lost 180 pounds (82 kg) after stomach surgery.

Elisa Johnson, born and adopted by Magic and Cookie in 1995, mostly stays out of the spotlight. Still, this young college student is also becoming known for her chic style sense and has appeared at numerous events in the world of fashion and on social media.

Magic Johnson and his family at a charity event in Beverly Hills, California, in 2014. From left: son André, André's wife Lisa, Magic's wife Cookie, Magic, daughter Elisa, and son EJ.

Chapter 6
Magic Johnson Reinvented

In the mid-1980s, at the peak of his basketball career, Magic Johnson began focusing on another of his childhood dreams. As a little kid in Lansing, Michigan, he was inspired by a pair of wealthy African-American businessmen, with their fancy homes and luxury cars. He decided he wanted to be a successful businessperson—just like them. In 1987, he launched Magic Johnson Enterprises to make that dream a reality.

Off-Court Magic

The first venture launched by Magic Johnson Enterprises was a sporting goods store. It was supposed to have become a chain of stores. Instead, it was a flop.

Never one to give up, Magic (who uses his given name, Earvin, in the business world) went back to the drawing board. He and his business partners soon came up with a new idea—inner-city movie theaters.

"I think Magic Johnson is just wonderful because he tries to make people happy. And that's the difference between Magic and Earvin. Earvin is a very serious guy, and a guy who is a focused person. Magic is fun, happy-go-lucky and he loves to make people happy."

Earvin "Magic" Johnson, in a 2005 interview

Earvin remembered how much he had loved going to the movies with his parents and siblings when he was a kid. He recognized, too, that this was no longer an option for many kids who lived in an urban setting. Some neighborhoods had become dangerous sites of violence and gang activity. They lacked safe, modern entertainment venues—and other services—for families.

Earvin set out to revive these "run-down and neglected" African-American parts of town. He knew they offered untapped business opportunities. He also knew it was cheap to buy property in these densely populated areas, compared to property in the suburbs.

"This wasn't just about me selling something and making money," said Earvin. "[It] was about entertaining people and providing something of value to the community, something that had been lost."

With that in mind, in 1995, the first Magic Johnson Theater opened its doors in the notorious South Central area of Los Angeles. (The neighborhood had been the site of disturbances and violence in 1992 after four police officers had been cleared of charges of using excessive force in the arrest and beating of motorist Rodney King.) The movie house was such a success that within a few years, a string of Magic Johnson Theaters opened in inner-city neighborhoods across the country.

Earvin's vision didn't stop there, though. In 1998, he partnered with Starbucks to open 125 coffee shops in urban, mostly African-American, neighborhoods across the nation. Again, he was successful. Next, he brought fast food chains, family restaurants, and fitness clubs to neighborhoods thought to be unsafe and therefore poor business risks.

Through these initiatives, Earvin became a leader in revitalizing urban areas, by providing contemporary shops and services— but these urban upgrades were just the beginning for this savvy businessman.

More of That Magic Touch

Today, the former basketball star and CEO of Magic Johnson Enterprises has his hands in real estate, investment management, insurance companies, the restaurant industry, retail stores, airports, and broadcasting. (He sold Magic Johnson Theaters in 2004, and the chain of Starbucks stores in 2010.)

He is a motivational speaker, an NBA commentator, a film and TV producer—and even though he sold his stake in the Los Angeles Lakers in 2010, Earvin remains a sports team owner.

In 2012, he and a group of investors purchased the Los Angeles Dodgers major league baseball team, along with Dodgers Stadium, for a record $2 billion. Earvin also owns shares in minor league baseball and basketball teams. In 2014, he became co-owner

Magic lets loose with one of his trademark laughs at a convention center in Anaheim, California. He and his business associates are on their way to a meeting with Best Buy executives. There, they will share ideas on opening stores in neighborhoods where many firms might be reluctant to do business.

New Los Angeles Dodgers co-owner Magic Johnson accompanies Sharon Robinson (left) and Rachel Robinson onto the field for the ceremonial first pitch of a game at Dodger Stadium in May 2012. Rachel and Sharon are the widow and daughter of the late, great Brooklyn Dodger and civil rights pioneer, Jackie Robinson.

of the Los Angeles Sparks of the Women's National Basketball Association (WNBA). In that same year, he also became co-owner of a major league soccer team—the Los Angeles Football Club—scheduled to begin play in 2018. He has also announced plans to bring a National Football League team to Los Angeles.

A Star of a Different Stripe

Magic Johnson isn't just a star on the basketball court and in the boardroom. He's also a star in the pop culture world. In 1993, he won a Grammy Award for Best Spoken Word Album, for the audiobook version of his bestseller *What You Can Do to Avoid AIDS*. He also has a star on the Hollywood Walk of Fame, in honor of his Magic Johnson Theaters.

Still Going Strong

No matter what else he does in his post-NBA life, Earvin "Magic" Johnson continues on his mission to raise awareness about HIV/AIDS.

It's important to note that Magic has not been cured of the HIV virus. Today, there are about 30 medications available to manage the illness and prevent it from developing into AIDS—but there is no cure.

Still, a quarter century after learning he was HIV-positive, the former basketballer continues to live a healthy, active lifestyle—thanks to a combination of smart physical activity, daily medications, the love and support of his family, and an upbeat, generous outlook.

"Simply by living, he [has proven] that an HIV infection was no longer an automatic death sentence. It is not possible to overstate how badly that message was needed in the minority communities that had been affected most severely, yet were, as always, least well served by the public-health system."

Michael Specter, *The New Yorker*, 2014

Magic Johnson greets service members on November 11, 2011. The occasion is a Carrier Classic basketball game, played on the flight deck of an aircraft carrier, between men's teams from the University of North Carolina and Michigan State University. (North Carolina won, 67–55.)

AIDS ADVANCES OVER THE YEARS

When Magic Johnson was diagnosed with HIV, there was only one drug available to treat the infection, and AIDS was the number-one killer of American men between age 25 and 44.

Today, thanks to advances in medical research, there are more than 30 drugs available, and more than 1.2 million Americans are living with HIV. When managed well, HIV may now be considered a chronic illness, one that persists over a long time or constantly recurs, and not a death sentence. A recent study showed that people with HIV who follow doctors' orders and properly take their meds aren't likely to die any earlier than their non-infected counterparts.

That's not to say HIV/AIDS isn't dangerous. Just because Magic Johnson and others are HIV-positive and living well doesn't mean it's not a serious illness.

"People look at [Magic], and say, 'Hey, it's OK to get HIV because [he's] living with it,'" stated a 2011 *CBS News* article. "That is the wrong message. The message is take care of yourself. Don't get it. But if you do, do the proper things to stay alive."

Probably the most important preventing tool for HIV is education. This includes education about safe sex practices and avoiding the risks of injected, or intravenous (IV), drug use. There are so many dangers associated with drug use, including HIV/AIDS, that it is difficult to address all of them quickly and simply. Seeking counseling and HIV testing are among the most important strategies for dealing with the use of IV drugs.

The safest path in practicing safe sex is to abstain from, or avoid, sexual activity. For some, this might mean waiting until you are an adult. At any age, safe sex should include understanding the risks and being careful to avoid exposing yourself, or those you care about, to those risks.

It's also important to get tested for HIV if there's any chance you have contracted it. Because some people are nervous about going to a clinic, home-testing kits are now available.

The red ribbon is a universally recognized symbol of AIDS awareness and shows support for people with HIV/AIDS.

Since stepping away from his professional hoops career, the legendary athlete's magic touch has reached into so many different realms that he is no longer considered merely a basketball icon.

Certainly, Magic is known as the hoops wizard who brought his big smile and sense of fun to the court, and the MVP point guard who helped a failing NBA rebound to become the show it is today. But he is also admired as the successful businessman who remembers his roots, and the vulnerable family man who changed the world's perception of HIV/AIDS.

Whether on the basketball court, in the boardroom, at a fund-raiser, or as an AIDS activist and educator, Earvin Johnson Jr. has lived up to his nickname over and over again. He is Magic.

Chronology

August 14, 1959 Earvin Johnson Jr. is born in Lansing, Michigan.

1969 Plays on a school basketball team for the first time, in fifth grade.

1971 Meets one of his basketball idols, Lew Alcindor, who soon changes his name to Kareem Abdul-Jabbar.

1973 Becomes one of about 100 African-American students bused to formerly all-white Everett High School; joins Everett Vikings basketball team.

1974 Sports reporter Fred Stabley Jr. gives Earvin the nickname "Magic."

1977 Magic and Everett H.S. win state high school basketball championship; holds press conference in spring to announce he has decided to attend Michigan State University in fall; joins Michigan State Spartans basketball team; meets Earleatha "Cookie" Kelly, who later becomes his wife.

1978 Featured on cover of *Sports Illustrated* in November; magazine names him one of top-ten sophomore college basketball players in America.

1979 Spartans win NCAA championship for first time in team's history; Magic drafted by Los Angeles Lakers.

1980 Lakers win NBA championship; Magic named series MVP.

1981 Magic's first child, André, is born and lives in Lansing with the baby's mother; Lakers owner Jerry Buss signs Magic to a 25-year, $25 million contract, the longest, richest contract in American sports history at the time.

1982 Lakers win NBA championship; Magic named post-season MVP for second time.

1984 L.A. Lakers meet Boston Celtics in NBA finals; first time Magic and his rival Larry Bird have met in a championship game since college; Lakers lose series.

1985 Boston and L.A. face each other in NBA finals again; Lakers win.

1987 Boston and L.A. meet in NBA finals for third time; Lakers win; Magic named finals MVP for third time and season MVP for first time; launches his company, Magic Johnson Enterprises.

1988 Lakers defeat Detroit Pistons in NBA finals to become NBA champions for fifth time in Magic's career.

1989, 1990 Wins NBA season MVPs.

1991 Magic and Cookie marry in September, 14 years after they first met; November 7: Magic holds press conference to announce that he has tested HIV-positive and is retiring immediately from NBA; within two weeks of press conference, launches

Magic Johnson Foundation to raise money for HIV/AIDS education and research; President George Bush invites Magic to join National Commission on AIDS.

1992 Returns to basketball to play in NBA All-Star Game in February; awarded game MVP trophy; jersey (32) is retired by Lakers; son Earvin III, known as "EJ," is born; earns gold medal with U.S. "Dream Team" at Olympic Games in August; in September, announces he is coming out of retirement; resigns from National Commission on AIDS in frustration over government's lack of action on AIDS crisis; November 3: after debate over health risks to other players and to Magic himself, holds press conference to announce second retirement from NBA; publishes two books, *What You Can Do to Avoid AIDS* and his autobiography, *My Life*.

1993 Earns Grammy Award for Best Spoken Word Album based on his book *What You Can Do to Avoid AIDS*.

1994 Becomes interim coach for Lakers; quits after 16 games; buys shares in the team; founds the Magic Johnson All-Stars exhibition team.

1995 Magic and Cookie adopt a baby girl named Elisa; Magic Johnson Enterprises opens first of five Magic Johnson Theaters.

1996 Sells his Lakers shares; joins team as player for final three months of the 1995–1996 regular season; Lakers lose to Houston in first round of NBA playoffs; again announces retirement from NBA and re-purchases his part-ownership shares in Lakers.

1998 Partners with Starbucks to open 125 coffee shops in inner-city neighborhoods; launches *The Magic Hour*, a talk show with such poor ratings that it is canceled after two months.

2001 Honored with a star on Hollywood Walk of Fame.

2002 Inducted into Basketball Hall of Fame for NBA career.

2004 Sells Magic Johnson Theater chain.

2008 Writes book about his business experiences, *32 Ways to Be a Champion in Business*.

2009 Co-authors book, *When the Game Was Ours*, with Larry Bird

2010 Sells his shares in Lakers, but stays on as unpaid vice president; sells Starbucks stores; inducted into Basketball Hall of Fame for second time, as a member of the 1992 Olympic Dream Team.

2012 Becomes part-owner of Los Angeles Dodgers baseball team and Dodgers Stadium.

2014 Becomes part owner of Los Angeles Football Club, a major league soccer team scheduled to begin play in 2018; given *Sports Illustrated* Legacy Award.

2016 Named greatest point guard in NBA history by sports network ESPN.

Glossary

advocate Someone who publicly supports an idea, organization, person, or cause

agility The ability to move quickly, easily, and gracefully

assembly line A series of workers and machines that build a product, in sequence; each machine or worker performs the same task over and over again, to build a series of identical items of the product

callous Insensitive or lacking concern for the feelings of others

colored A term, now usually considered outdated and socially offensive in North America, to describe someone who is wholly or partly of black descent

correspondent A reporter

custodian A janitor, caretaker

desegregate To open a school, or other facility, to people of all races; to end a policy of segregation, usually on the basis of race

diabetes A disease that causes high levels of glucose (a type of sugar) in the blood

dribble To bounce a basketball while walking or running with it

echelon A level of achievement or reputation in an organization or in society

entourage A group of people who surround and usually support an important person

exuberance Excitement, energy, overflowing happiness

foreman The supervisor, or person in charge, in a workplace

forward One of two positions on a basketball team—power forward and small forward—that require a versatile player who is a strong scorer, rebounder, and defender

free throw The chance to shoot the ball into the basket and score a single point after a foul has been committed, without being blocked by an opposing player

Great Depression A period of international economic crisis that started in October 1929 and lasted through the 1930s

heyday The period of a person's greatest success, achievement, or popularity

idle Doing nothing, lacking purpose

initiative A new plan, process, or business

inner city The usually older and more heavily populated, often poorer, central section of a city

integrated Desegregated, mixed

interim Temporary; intended as short term until a permanent replacement or solution can be found

irony A situation whose outcome is the opposite of what was expected, and which may therefore be considered unusual or amusing

lanky Tall and lean, sometimes suggesting scrawny

notorious Famous or well known, typically for a negative reason

nurture To care for, or encourage, someone's growth or development

pick-up game A spontaneous basketball game, usually with no referee; teams are chosen on the spot from players who are available

point guard In basketball, the player who calls the plays on the court and sets up scoring opportunities; must possess strong passing, ball handling, and decision-making skills

press conference A scheduled meeting with journalists at which an announcement is made and reporters may ask questions

rebound In basketball, a recovery of possession of the ball following a missed shot

recruit To persuade someone to do something; in sports it usually means getting someone interested in joining a team or attending a university

revitalize To bring new life and energy to something that is weak or failing

revive To bring back to life

roster A list of individuals or groups

run and gun A fast-paced, high-scoring style of basketball that features fewer set plays, a high number of shots taken, and usually a higher-scoring game on both sides

Sabbath A religious day of rest and worship

savvy Clever, wise

segregation The enforced separation of different racial groups

sleight-of-hand Quick and clever hand movements, often used in magic tricks

stoic Not inclined to show feelings or emotions

telecommunications Communications via telephone, telegraph, cable, broadcasting, digital technology, or other electronic means

tolerant Open-minded, accepting of opinions and ideas different from one's own

unsolicited Not asked for; given or done voluntarily

venture A bold, daring, or risky business or other undertaking

Further Information

Books

Bird, Larry, Earvin "Magic" Johnson, with Jackie MacMullan. *When the Game Was Ours.* New York: Houghton Mifflin Harcourt, 2009.

Johnson, Earvin "Magic," with William Novak *My Life*. New York: Fawcett Books, 1992.

Lace, William W. *The Los Angeles Lakers Basketball Team* (Great Sports Teams). Springfield, NJ: Enslow Publishers, 1998.

Video/DVDs

The Announcement (DVD). ESPN, NBA Entertainment, 2012. ESPN documentary about Magic Johnson, his HIV announcement, and his post-NBA life.

Magic & Bird: A Courtship of Rivals (DVD). HBO Studios, 2010. This 90-minute documentary examines two of basketball's most famous superstars when their careers made them both the most intense of rivals and, later, the best of friends.

Magic Johnson: Always Showtime (DVD). Team Marketing, 2006. Narrated by actor Danny Glover, this two-disc, seven-hour documentary features tons of visuals and information about Magic's basketball career, including his championship days at Everett High School and Michigan State, and the Showtime era with the L.A. Lakers. Three of his greatest NBA games are featured, as well as his number retirement ceremony and several interviews with Magic himself.

Magic Johnson Top 10 Showtime Moments (online video). nba.com, 2015. A three-minute collection of select moments from Magic Johnson's Hall of Fame career, highlighting the flash and skill of his performance and the joy he brought to fans in the stands. Among the highlight reel moments are fun, enthusiastic bits from interviews with Magic and former Lakers coach Pat Riley. Available online: **http://www.nba.com/video/channels/top_plays/2015/08/14/20150814-**

magic-johnson-top10-showtime-moments.nba/
Showtime at the Forum (online video). nba.com, 2009. More video from the NBA's online website showing off the innovative style of basketball that Magic, Johnson and the Los Angeles Lakers were known for during the 1980s. This video includes footage from *Magic Johnson Top 10 Showtime Moments*, but it also features clips of other members of the Showtime Lakers, plus comments and cameo appearances by some of the celebrities who celebrated in the stands. You can find it at the following link online:
http://www.nba.com/video/channels/nba_tv/2009/08/10/ nba_090810_magic_showtime.nba/index.html

In addition to the links from nba.com listed above, you can type "Magic Johnson" into the "search" window on the nba.com home page for dozens more short films related to the superstar point guard and the Lakers of his era.

Websites

www.nba.com
Everything you need to know about the NBA, past and present, is on the NBA website. Some of the links to videos about Magic Johnson are listed above. Here are a few key links to online stories and articles about Magic and other fascinating players and events in the history of the National Basketball Association:
http://www.nba.com/history/
http://www.nba.com/encyclopedia/playoff_edition.html
http://www.nba.com/history/legends/magic-johnson/
http://www.nba.com/history/players/johnsonm_bio.html

http://www.hoophall.com/
This is the link to the Naismith Memorial Basketball Hall of Fame. It's located in Springfield, Massachusetts, where basketball began.

https://naismithbasketballfoundation.com/
This is the home page of the Naismith Basketball Foundation. Here, you will find information about the founder of the game, James Naismith, and the museum in his hometown of Almonte, Ontario, Canada.

http://www.eschooltoday.com/hiv-aids/hiv-aids-introduction.html
This page, titled *What Every Young Person Should Know on … HIV AIDS*, is a kid-friendly overview of HIV, the condition that affects Magic Johnson, and AIDS.

Index

About the Author

Diane Dakers was born and raised in Toronto and now makes her home in Victoria, British Columbia. She has written two fiction and 15 nonfiction books for young people. Diane loves finding and telling stories about what makes people tick—be they world-changers like Earvin "Magic" Johnson, or lesser-known folks like you and me.